H E A T H
MIDDLE LEVEL
LITERATURE

Unconquered

Survivors never give up, no matter what kinds of challenges
they face. What can you learn about survival by reading
about the challenges others have faced?

A U T H O R S

Donna Alvermann
Linda Miller Cleary
Kenneth Donelson
Donald Gallo
Alice Haskins
J. Howard Johnston
John Lounsbury
Alleen Pace Nilsen
Robert Pavlik
Jewell Parker Rhodes
Alberto Alvaro Ríos
Sandra Schurr
Lyndon Searfoss
Julia Thomason
Max Thompson
Carl Zon

D.C. Heath and Company
Lexington, Massachusetts / Toronto, Ontario

STAFF CREDITS

EDITORIAL	Barbara A. Brennan, Susan Belt Cogley, DeVona Dors, Christopher Johnson, Rita M. Sullivan, Patricia B. Weiler
	Proofreading: JoAnne B. Sgroi
CONTRIBUTING WRITERS	Kathy Tuchman Glass, Jo Pitkin
SERIES DESIGN	Robin Herr
BOOK DESIGN	Caroline Bowden, Daniel Derdula, Susan Geer, Diana Maloney, Angela Sciaraffa, Bonnie Chayes Yousefian
	Art Editing: Carolyn Langley
PHOTOGRAPHY	*Series Photography Coordinator:* Carmen Johnson
	Photo Research Supervisor: Martha Friedman
	Photo Researchers: Wendy Enright, Linda Finigan, Po-yee McKenna, PhotoSearch, Inc., Gillian Speeth, Denise Theodores
	Assignment Photography Coordinators: Susan Doheny, Gayna Hoffman, Shawna Johnston
COMPUTER PREPRESS	Ricki Pappo, Kathy Meisl, Richard Curran, Michele Locatelli
PERMISSIONS	Dorothy B. McLeod
PRODUCTION	Patrick Connolly

Cover: *The Large Family* by Rene Magritte, circa 1947, Herscovici/Art Resource, N.Y.
Cover Design: Steve Snider

Published simultaneously in Canada

Printed in the United States of America

International Standard Book Number: 0-669-32111-7 (soft cover); 0-669-38179-9 (hard cover)
2 3 4 5 6 7 8 9 10-RRD-99 98 97 96 95 94

Middle Level Authors

Donna Alvermann, University of Georgia
Alice Haskins, Howard County Public Schools, Maryland
J. Howard Johnston, University of South Florida
John Lounsbury, Georgia College
Sandra Schurr, University of South Florida
Julia Thomason, Appalachian State University
Max Thompson, Appalachian State University
Carl Zon, California Assessment Collaborative

Literature and Language Arts Authors

Linda Miller Cleary, University of Minnesota
Kenneth Donelson, Arizona State University
Donald Gallo, Central Connecticut State University
Alleen Pace Nilsen, Arizona State University
Robert Pavlik, Cardinal Stritch College, Milwaukee
Jewell Parker Rhodes, Arizona State University
Alberto Alvaro Ríos, Arizona State University
Lyndon Searfoss, Arizona State University

Teacher Consultants

Suzanne Aubin, Patapsco Middle School, Ellicott City, Maryland
Judy Baxter, Newport News Public Schools, Newport News, Virginia
Saundra Bryn, Director of Research and Development, El Mirage, Arizona
Lorraine Gerhart, Elmbrook Middle School, Elm Grove, Wisconsin
Kathy Tuchman Glass, Burlingame Intermediate School, Burlingame, California
Lucretia Pannozzo, John Jay Middle School, Katonah, New York
Carol Schultz, Jerling Junior High, Orland Park, Illinois
Jeanne Siebenman, Grand Canyon University, Phoenix, Arizona
Gail Thompson, Garey High School, Pomona, California
Rufus Thompson, Grace Yokley School, Ontario, California
Tom Tufts, Conniston Middle School, West Palm Beach, Florida
Edna Turner, Harpers Choice Middle School, Columbia, Maryland
C. Anne Webb, Buerkle Junior High School, St. Louis, Missouri
Geri Yaccino, Thompson Junior High School, St. Charles, Illinois

CONTENTS

THE LITERATURE

Stairs, Provincetown Charles Demuth, 1920

ASKING BIG QUESTIONS ABOUT THE LITERATURE

PROJECTS

1 WRITING WORKSHOP

WRITE A RESEARCH PAPER 106-111

Examine survival challenges as you learn the techniques and skills necessary to write a research paper.

2 COOPERATIVE LEARNING

TAKE ME TO THE FAIR 112-113

Become familiar with various cultures as you and your classmates participate in a cultural fair.

3 HELPING YOUR COMMUNITY

AND JUSTICE FOR ALL 114-115

Develop a campaign to make people aware of injustice.

The Right Stuff

1 True or false?

- You can't live by bread alone.
- Love makes the world go round.
- A person's home is his or her castle.

  Food, shelter, and love are important ingredients in survival. But they are not the only ones. Work with a partner or in a group to answer the question, "What is necessary for survival?"

2 Survival means . . .

The boxes on this page contain some of the right stuff for survival. Study the ingredients in each box. What other ingredients can you add? Write your answers on a separate sheet of paper.

- Giving and receiving love

- Having opportunities to succeed

- Feeling safe and secure

- Having knowledge

- Having food, water, and shelter

- Being accepted by others

- Having friends

SURVIVAL

3 One Step at a Time

Imagine climbing a ladder like the one shown. Each rung on the ladder contains a survival ingredient. As you climb the ladder, you can take the ingredient on each rung with you. But the ladder is steep, and you're not sure you can reach the top. What will you place on the first rung of the ladder? What will you place on the next rung?

4 The Right Slot

Working alone or in small groups, create a survival ladder. First, identify the ingredients that you or your group consider important. Then place each ingredient on a rung. Put the most important ingredients at or near the bottom. Put those you may be able to do without further up. Be prepared to defend or explain your choices.

When you have finished, compare your ladder with others in your class. How are the ladders alike? How are they different?

Asking Big Questions About the Theme

What is survival?

The word *survive* comes from the Latin word *vivere*, meaning "to live." But survival is more than living. Survival implies the triumph of the spirit and the body over overwhelming obstacles. In your journal, summarize survival stories you've read about or heard about in the news. If appropriate, include survival situations faced by your family and friends. Use these situations to brainstorm for definitions of survival.

What does it take to survive?

Some people have almost everything they need or want. Others have the basics and a few extras that make their lives more pleasant. And still others have few, if any, of the basics of survival. What do *you* need to survive? What can you do without? Use a chart like the one shown to record your answers in your journal. Remember that your journal is private. You do not have to share your answers.

Things I Need	Things I Could Do Without

What kinds of survival challenges have different cultures faced?

People face survival challenges as individuals. But sometimes the survival of an entire group is threatened. For example, the arrival of Christopher Columbus and later Europeans threatened the survival of Native Americans. Working in small groups or as a class, make a chart like the one shown, of other groups whose survival has been challenged. Use your knowledge of history and current events to help you.

Group Survival	Challenges
Native Americans	Destruction of ways of life by European explorers

Why do people threaten one another's survival?

Have you ever been bullied or teased? If so, you may have asked, "What is wrong with me?" The answer is, "*Nothing* is wrong with you." The problem lies in the other person. In your journal, write down some imaginary or real situations in which one person threatens another. Then move on to a global perspective and think about historical situations in which one nation threatens another. Discuss these situations in small groups and then brainstorm to find reasons for the actions of the threatening nation.

NOW Think!

With a partner or in a small group, write other questions about survival in your journal. As you read the literature and complete the activities and projects that follow, consider answers for the Big Questions and your own questions.

LEWIS H. LATIMER

Unconquered and Unconquerable

What tho' I suffer through the years
Unnumbered wrongs, unnumbered fears
My soul doth still forbid me tears
Unconquered and unconquerable

What tho' my bed of thorns be made   5
What tho' my onward cruise be stayed
My soul soars upward undismayed
Unconquered and unconquerable

What tho' by chains confined I lie
What tho' by brutal hands I die   10
My soul will upward ever fly
Unconquered and unconquerable

I scorn the hand that did me wrong
Tho' suffering days and years be long
My soul still charts that deathless song   15
Unconquered and unconquerable

LEWIS H. LATIMER

Louis Howard Latimer [1848-1928] was born in Chelsea, Massachusetts. When he was fifteen years old, he was one of the first African Americans to enlist in the Union Navy.

An engineer and an inventor as well as a poet, he invented the first incandescent electric light bulb with a carbon filament. As an engineer for Edison Company, he supervised the first installation of electric lights in New York, Philadelphia, Montreal, and London.

His poetry is in a book called *Poems of Love and Life*.

FROM

THE GIRL IN THE WHITE SHIP

PETER TOWNSEND

After the defeat of South Vietnam by North Vietnam in 1975, the actions of the Communist regime made it necessary for many Vietnamese to flee their country in boats. This was particularly true for the ethnic Chinese, who were long established in the country. In fact, most of them were descended from ancestors who had arrived in Vietnam in the seventeenth and nineteenth centuries. What you will read next tells about such a family.

One day at the end of August, when the evening meal was finished and Co Ut,[1] the housekeeper, had gone home, Tinh[2] got up and quietly closed all the windows of the living room. The children wondered why, until he spoke to them in his calm voice: "Gather around, I have something to tell you." They came to him, and his voice became grave as he went on. "Listen. In about two weeks we are all going to escape, to leave our home forever and sail to Malaysia.[3] From there I'll contact our cousin Ly To[4] in Australia, which will be our new home. All the plans for the journey to Malaysia are made. There will be ninety people in the boat and we will leave at midnight on September twelfth, two nights before the full moon. By then the moon festival will have begun, so the curfew will be relaxed and we'll be able to move around with less danger from the police."

As Tinh talked, Le Mai[5] looked absently in front of her. She had known his plans for weeks and did not want to listen; she was thinking how hard it would be to leave behind her own and Tinh's widowed mothers and her sister Phuong.[6] The children, however, listened intently as Tinh continued: "You all know that the secret police have an eye on us. They have not bothered us seriously since they closed down the shop, but you must always remember that they or their informers may be watching and listening. They are the first danger to get by, though there will be others once we are at sea. The police, if they catch us, will put us in prison and then we'll be moved to a New Economic Zone. You little ones must not repeat a single word of what I have told you, even among yourselves. You go on as if you knew nothing."

The children's hearts beat faster as their father spoke. His voice, so calm and serious, made the danger feel more real. When he had

1. **Co Ut** [kō ùt]
2. **Tinh** [tēn]
3. **Malaysia** [mə lā′zhə]: a country in Southeast Asia, south of Vietnam.
4. **Ly To** [lē tō]
5. **Le Mai** [lā mäē]
6. **Phuong** [fwōng]

finished speaking the children were silent. They needed time for his words to sink in, to work on their minds. They reacted in their own fashion. Hue Hue's[7] one terror was that the police might catch them; she did not give a thought for the voyage, except that she longed for it to start. She could not help feeling sad at the idea of leaving, nor could she bring herself to believe that she would never again see her friends or their house, with all its memories. It hurt to think that she must leave her friends without even saying good-bye.

Trung,[8] like his mother, said little; his thoughts too were far away. He was thrilled at the promise of a new life in Australia. Forget the police, he thought to himself; and the voyage too. In a few months we will be there. As for Quang[9] and To,[10] they were chattering excitedly about the police; they dreaded them, but it would be exciting to give them the slip and then sail away across the sea to Malaysia. "Bet you'll be the first to be seasick," To laughed at Quang. "If you win I'll give you ten *dong*.[11] They won't be any good anyway where we're going."

For the children the next two weeks seemed endless. In class their thoughts would often wander to the secret their father had told them. The teacher would snap, "Pay attention, there, what do you think you're dreaming of?" At the beginning of the second week in September, the family gathered at midday in a nearby restaurant for a farewell party. There were those who were leaving—Tinh and Le Mai and the children; Le Mai's younger sister, the children's twenty-three-year-old Aunt Binh;[12] and their cousin Ly Tu Dan[13] of about the same age. And there were those who were being left—Le Mai's mother, her other sister, Phuong, and her brother and his wife, as well as Tinh's mother, his sister Ngan[14] and his two brothers. Phuong

---

7. **Hue Hue** [húā húā]
8. **Trung** [trùng]
9. **Quang** [kwäng]
10. **To** [tō]
11. *dong* [dông]
12. **Binh** [bēn]
13. **Ly Tu Dan** [lē tù dän]
14. **Ngan** [ngän]

had chosen the expensive menu: *cha gia*[15] (spring rolls), *mi*[16] (noodle soup), *nem nuong*[17] (brochette of beef), *bun tom*[18] (grilled prawns and noodles), and *chao gao*[19] (chicken and sticky rice)—all favorite dishes, which helped make the occasion seem festive. Yet not for an instant could any of them forget that this was the last time they would all be together.

The meal over, they walked to the home of Le Mai's mother for the final farewell. Tinh spoke the last words to those remaining behind. "This is the last time that we will see one another. Within a week you will get word that we have left. We ourselves will send word from Malaysia. Pray for us; we shall always pray for you." As they embraced for the last time, they were all in tears.

When at last September 12 arrived, the children were packed off to school as usual. If the housekeeper felt that their good-byes were unusually affectionate, her placid face betrayed no surprise. As the last class of the afternoon broke up, Hue Hue felt that she could not deceive her friends to the point of saying the usual, "Good-bye, see you tomorrow." She waved and called out "Good-bye," hardly able to believe that it was forever.

A little before then, a man had brought word to Tinh from Uncle Ba[20] that he was to leave the house at 6 P.M. sharp and go to warn another family in his neighborhood to rendezvous forthwith at the marketplace, Ninh Kieu,[21] beside the small river Cau Cui.[22] Tinh's own family were to gather at the same spot. The departure was on.

At midday, as the housekeeper made ready to return to her home, Le Mai stopped her and Tinh said, "We are going to leave very soon. Don't come back, we shall say good-bye to you now." As she had

15. *cha gia* [tyä yä]
16. *mi* [mē]
17. *nem nuong* [nem nwong]
18. *bun tom* [bún tom]
19. *chao gao* [tyäw gäw]
20. **Ba** [bä]
21. **Ninh Kieu** [nin kyiw]
22. **Cau Cui** [käw kuy]

done earlier that morning with the children, the housekeeper showed no surprise. They talked for some minutes, and then as they took leave, Tinh said: "Come back after we have left and help yourself to anything you want from the house. But not before five days after you hear we have gone." Five days. By then the family should be in Malaysia.

The children were all home by 4 P.M. Le Mai gave them rice and sweet pork, telling them: "Eat all you can. We'll be going hungry for the next week." When they had eaten she said to them, "Now go quietly to your rooms and change." Each of the children and their parents had set aside some old, worn clothes in which they could pass as fisherfolk. Hue Hue slipped out of her clean school uniform and changed into a grubby striped blouse and a flowery-pattern pajama, over which she pulled an old pair of black cotton trousers. She had also kept a checked jacket, threadbare at the elbows, to wear during the cool nights at sea. On her feet she wore leather sandals with a strap over the toes. Le Mai's outfit was similar. The boys had taken off their clean white shirts and carefully creased blue shorts and thrown them on the bed. Giggling, they pulled on the disguises that Tinh had procured for them and himself, the salt-stained nondescript shirt, black trousers, and typical fisherman's sandals.

Warned by Uncle Ba's unfortunate encounter earlier with the police, the family took nothing with them. The police knew too well that people carrying luggage were people bent on escaping. But each member of the family now discreetly concealed a quantity of U.S. dollar bills that Tinh had obtained on the black market; the money might come in handy for bribing the police. Tinh himself had hidden fifteen ounces troy of gold and five hundred-dollar bills in a belt around his waist. Le Mai, Aunt Binh, cousin Dan,[23] and the three boys each had two hundred- dollar bills hidden in their clothing. To Hue Hue, Tinh had entrusted, besides two hundred-dollar bills, a solid gold necklace, which she wore beneath the buttoned-up collar of her blouse.

23. **Dan** [dän]

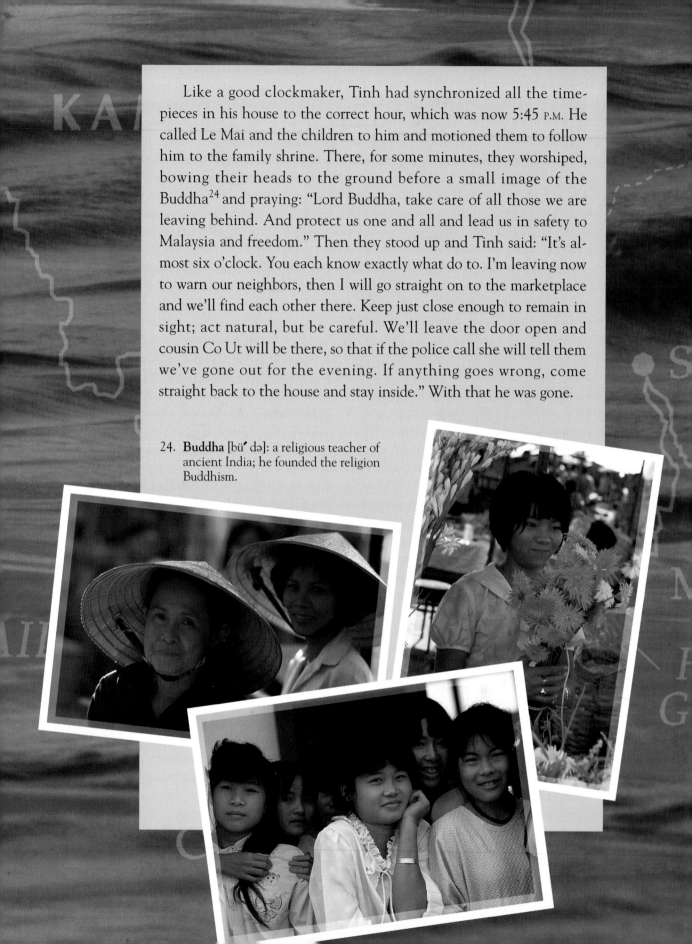

Like a good clockmaker, Tinh had synchronized all the time-pieces in his house to the correct hour, which was now 5:45 P.M. He called Le Mai and the children to him and motioned them to follow him to the family shrine. There, for some minutes, they worshiped, bowing their heads to the ground before a small image of the Buddha[24] and praying: "Lord Buddha, take care of all those we are leaving behind. And protect us one and all and lead us in safety to Malaysia and freedom." Then they stood up and Tinh said: "It's almost six o'clock. You each know exactly what do to. I'm leaving now to warn our neighbors, then I will go straight on to the marketplace and we'll find each other there. Keep just close enough to remain in sight; act natural, but be careful. We'll leave the door open and cousin Co Ut will be there, so that if the police call she will tell them we've gone out for the evening. If anything goes wrong, come straight back to the house and stay inside." With that he was gone.

24. **Buddha** [bü′ də]: a religious teacher of ancient India; he founded the religion Buddhism.

It was Hue Hue's turn to leave next. Before she did so, she ran back to her bedroom. Standing in the doorway, she glanced around, fixing in her mind the pale blue walls covered with photos of her family and friends and of her favorite actress Chan Chan.[25] On the shelf above her bed were stacked her table-tennis paddles and on the bed itself, tidily folded, her neat school uniform, white shirt and blue pleated skirt, with a heap of schoolbooks. On the pillow reclined her doll, wearing the new shirt and blue jeans she had just made for it. Good-bye, all of you and everything, she thought, and had to force back the tears. Then, firmly, thirteen-year-old Hue Hue shut the door behind her, closed it on her life in Vietnam. The odor of sweet pork and rice hanging about the house made her think: No more good things like that for a while.

A fond pat but no tears for the dog, Dolly, and Hue Hue was standing by the open front door with her mother and brothers. "See you all at the marketplace," she said. "Be careful." She turned and began walking toward Ninh Kieu, the marketplace, a half-mile away. A few minutes after her came Trung, then Quang, each taking a slightly different route. Finally Le Mai left with her youngest boy, To, and her sister Binh. As arranged, Le Mai had left the front door unlocked.

Hue Hue and her family, with the rest of the ninety people intent on escaping that night, were but a few of the hundreds converging on the Ninh Kieu for the moon-festival celebrations.[26] Hue Hue walked at a leisurely pace, yet every fiber of her small body was taut. This was another game, an escaping game, which, like running or table tennis, would need all her wits and determination if she was to win it. She noticed with some perplexity that her sandals seemed unusually heavy. Every now and again they slipped off her feet. She did not discover till later that Tinh had inserted five *la*—gold leaves—between the upper and lower soles, which added two ounces to the weight of each sandal.

At about half-past six Hue Hue reached the market. Dusk was falling; the night was warm and not a breath of wind stirred the

25. **Chan Chan** [tyän tyän]
26. **moon-festival celebrations**: special festival for children.

palm trees. Stars were beginning to shine in a cloudless, darkening sky; festive music played throughout the marketplace. That night was one of the most beautiful that Hue Hue could remember. She loitered for a while near the food shops that, with the bus company's ticket office, were the only establishments open. She noticed a few policemen strolling among the crowds but did not feel afraid of them. The moon festival was a festival for children, and so there were many of them in the marketplace, each with a lantern, each eating candy and moon-cake that made Hue Hue's mouth water, while their parents greeted their friends, chatted, and laughed. The moon festival seemed to have put everybody back into a good mood.

Scanning the crowds for the rest of the family, Hue Hue had no difficulty in spotting them in the glare of the gaslights; each made a sign of mutual recognition; then, still keeping their distance, they moved toward the bank of the Cau Cui. Hue Hue sat down on the ground at the riverbank, and began to chat with her brother Trung, her young Aunt Binh, and her cousin Dan.

About twenty paces away, she could just make out her father and mother seated on a bench with Quang and To. They too were chatting quietly. Tinh had just remarked to Le Mai: "It is hard to believe that fifteen years ago, on this very spot, we opened a fine shop, and now we are refugees fleeing to save our lives." Hue Hue's thoughts were running on the same theme.

On the river, boats and sampans[27] kept coming and going, ferrying people and vehicles to and fro from one end of National Route 4 to where it began again on the opposite

27. **sampans** [sam′panz]: small boats with oars, a single sail, and a cabin made of mats.

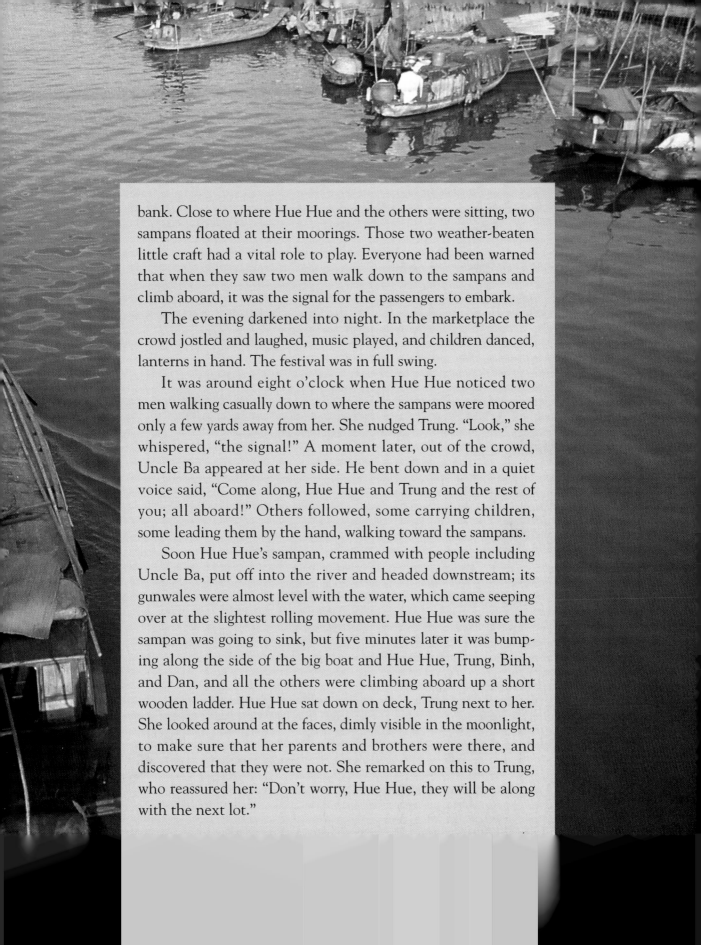

bank. Close to where Hue Hue and the others were sitting, two sampans floated at their moorings. Those two weather-beaten little craft had a vital role to play. Everyone had been warned that when they saw two men walk down to the sampans and climb aboard, it was the signal for the passengers to embark.

The evening darkened into night. In the marketplace the crowd jostled and laughed, music played, and children danced, lanterns in hand. The festival was in full swing.

It was around eight o'clock when Hue Hue noticed two men walking casually down to where the sampans were moored only a few yards away from her. She nudged Trung. "Look," she whispered, "the signal!" A moment later, out of the crowd, Uncle Ba appeared at her side. He bent down and in a quiet voice said, "Come along, Hue Hue and Trung and the rest of you; all aboard!" Others followed, some carrying children, some leading them by the hand, walking toward the sampans.

Soon Hue Hue's sampan, crammed with people including Uncle Ba, put off into the river and headed downstream; its gunwales were almost level with the water, which came seeping over at the slightest rolling movement. Hue Hue was sure the sampan was going to sink, but five minutes later it was bumping along the side of the big boat and Hue Hue, Trung, Binh, and Dan, and all the others were climbing aboard up a short wooden ladder. Hue Hue sat down on deck, Trung next to her. She looked around at the faces, dimly visible in the moonlight, to make sure that her parents and brothers were there, and discovered that they were not. She remarked on this to Trung, who reassured her: "Don't worry, Hue Hue, they will be along with the next lot."

Minutes went by. The second sampan, followed some moments later by Uncle Ba's with another load of passengers, came alongside. Carefully, Hue Hue searched the face of every passenger, until the last one stepped on deck. Still no sign of her parents and brothers. By now, she was so worried that she called out to Uncle Ba, who just then was climbing back down the ladder into his sampan. "Where are my parents and my brothers?" she asked, almost crying. Uncle Ba called back, "Don't worry, Hue Hue, I'll bring them along with the next lot." Then he and his sampan disappeared upstream into the darkness.

As he pulled in toward the riverbank at the marketplace, something looked amiss to Uncle Ba. The sampan drifted closer to the riverbank. Then, to his consternation, he saw that one of the waiting passengers was being questioned by a policeman, automatic rifle in hand. He saw Tinh standing a pace away from them. Ba stepped ashore and from a safe distance waited to see what would happen.

Tinh, meanwhile, despite the gold and dollar bills he carried on him, decided that this was not the moment to try bribing the police. His courage deserting at the thought that he, too, might be questioned and searched, he began to tremble visibly. Le Mai did the same, while the two little boys just stood there, petrified. They heard the policeman ask the man, "What are you all doing, hanging around here?" and the man's unhurried answer, "We are waiting to buy bus tickets to return to our homes in the country." The policeman appeared satisfied and walked away. As he did so, Tinh and his family and all the other fugitives, the 40 of them who remained ashore, made haste to disperse, disappearing under the palm trees, fading into the shadows. For them the riverbank at Ninh Kieu had become a decidedly unhealthy place.

As Tinh hurried away, half-running with his family, he passed within a few feet of his friend Ba. With so many people about, Ba could only speak in a loud whisper. "Come on, Tinh," he urged. "If you are coming, come now or it will be too late. I'm leaving." Ba was about to add, "Hue Hue and Trung are already aboard," when Tinh cut him short. "How can I possibly come with you," he pleaded, "and leave my two older children behind?" Without giving Ba a chance to explain, he rushed off into the dark with Le Mai and the two little boys.

Uncle Ba turned back toward his sampan. It was no longer there. He made for one of the waiting ferry-sampans, climbed into it, and pressed forty *dong,* instead of the usual two, into the hand of the astonished boatman. "Take it and keep your mouth shut," he ordered. "Row me downstream until I tell you to stop." Five minutes later the confused and frightened Uncle Ba was aboard the boat. To a young man who sat counting the passengers as they boarded Ba hissed, "How many?" "Fifty including you," the man replied. "All right. Pass the word around that we're leaving this instant. The police have discovered us." As he spoke, Ba fumbled with the engine controls, found the starter button, and pushed it. The diesel motor spluttered into life, then settled down, turning over steadily. "Cast off," ordered Ba, and called for Chu Nhi.[28] "Chu Nhi, where are you? Come and take over!" But Chu Nhi, who knew all about motors, especially this one, and was able to steer a compass course, was still on dry land, his pocket compass in his shirt pocket. Chu Nhi had missed the boat and there was not a soul on board competent to sail it.

In the wheelhouse Uncle Ba, his nerves taut, peered forward until his nose nearly touched the glass window. Next to him stood Trung, who Ba had told to stand by as messenger and lookout. Easing the boat away from its hidden moorings, Ba headed her carefully down the Cau Cui and into the broad waters of the Hau Giang,[29] the river that led down to the sea. From his brief war service in navy riverboats, Ba knew he could get the boat that far—he did not allow his thoughts to wander further. He must concentrate, get safely through the river traffic, keep a sharp lookout for the river police. He could see no reason why a riverboat with most of its fifty passengers hidden below deck should attract attention. All the same he warned Trung, "Keep your eyes skinned."

28. **Chu Nhi** [tyŭ nē]
29. **Hau Giang** [häw gyäng]

Soon Ba began to relax a little and it was then that he became conscious of a commotion below deck, sounds of wailing and moaning. "Go and see what's the matter," Ba told Trung, who disappeared. A few minutes later he was back. "It's the families who've been split up. They're going nearly mad. There's a girl of twelve who's crying and crying because her parents have been left behind. Other people are calling for their wives or their husbands and children." Ba said nothing, but continued through the glass of the wheelhouse. He was aware of a disturbing feeling that the boat, from the moment she got under way, was to be an unhappy one.

Trung had been able to have a few words with Hue Hue. Neither of them yet quite realized the drama of their situation. They had often talked about escaping alone. Well, this was it. They were completely on their own, cut off from their family. Trung said, "Get some sleep, Hue Hue," and went to join Ba in the wheelhouse. Below, on one of the wooden planks that had been laid on the cross-members of the boat, Hue Hue dozed, wedged tightly between two other people and maddeningly aware that she was being devoured by mosquitoes. Then she fell asleep, slumped against one of her neighbors. Occasionally she awoke and shifted herself from one uncomfortable position to another. Through a tiny porthole she saw palm trees go by and knew that the boat was still sailing down the river.

Tinh had shepherded his family safely through the dark back to the house. He opened the door and his cousin Co Ut, astonished, asked, "Why have you come back?" "The police," replied Tinh, quickly adding, "and Trung and Hue Hue. They're not back?" "Not yet," said Co Ut, "but they must be on their way." Tinh, Le Mai, and the boys, still feeling frightened, went to the sitting room. A few minutes later they heard the door open. "Must be them." But the two people at the door were friends of Tinh, and during the next twenty minutes more friends arrived. All were members of the escape group who lived near the police station and dared not go home. Tinh and Le Mai welcomed them mechanically, asking each one, "Have you seen Trung and Hue?" No one had seen either of the two children.

Tinh's clocks were all striking midnight; their concerted chimes nearly drove him mad, for they told him that three hours had passed since he last saw Ba, and that Trung and Hue Hue were still missing. Where could they be? Arrested? If so, he would find out tomorrow. Still at the moon festival? Tinh dismissed the idea. Those two loved to have fun, but they would never have disobeyed his instruction to return home should anything go wrong. Then he remembered the words that Ba had called after him: "Come on, Tinh, I'm leaving." Were his children with Ba? He spoke to Le Mai: "I think they must have left with Uncle Ba and the rest. Perhaps he'll turn back, then we can join them tomorrow." But Le Mai was not to be consoled by such a frail hope. She had been on the verge of breaking down since they returned to the house, and now through her tears she reproached Tinh. "You should never have allowed the children to get into such terrible danger." Tinh, venturing a last hope, replied, "But if they are with Ba, they should be safe enough."

When Tinh, exhausted, finally stretched out on his bed, it was nearly 3 A.M., six hours since the boat had left. He was now sure that Hue Hue and Trung were in it. Alone with his thoughts in the dark, his optimism vanished. When, if ever, would he see them again? He turned over and cried quietly to himself. In their beds Le Mai and the two little boys were crying too. No one slept that night.

Next morning Tinh's uninvited guests left his house and slipped back to their own, but others came to call on him. Tinh was well known in Cantho.[30] "We saw you down at the river last night," they said, eager for gossip. "Were you trying to escape?" Tinh, putting on a brave face, replied as politely as he could: "How could I have been trying to escape since I'm still here?" All the same, the gossip spread. It was bound, sooner or later, to reach the ears of the police. Meanwhile, Tinh and Le Mai forced themselves to carry on as if it were just another day. Quang and To were sent off to school, but not

30. **Cantho** [kän tōʹ]

before Tinh told them: "If you are asked about your brother and sister, say that they have gone to Saigon."[31]

Half a dozen boys and girls, friends of Trung and Hue Hue, came to the house that evening. They—and others, no doubt, including the teachers—had noticed their absence in class; that must mean that they had escaped. Tinh led them inside to Le Mai and the boys. One of Hue Hue's friends, Hoa,[32] spoke for the rest. "We want to say how sorry we are and how much we all miss them. We shall go to the temple and pray that they will return safely to you." But not all the sympathy of their own and the children's friends could alter the cruel reality of the two empty places at table. As Le Mai later said: "We ate rice mixed with tears."

Three nights after the children's disappearance, Tinh, sleeping fitfully, had a strange dream. He saw Trung and Hue Hue on a rock in the middle of the sea. They were both naked and were clearly alive. Then, bending over him, Tinh saw an aged saffron-robed[33] priest, with drooping mustaches and a long white beard. "How many children have you?" asked the bonze, and Tinh replied, "Four, but two are away." "Yes," said the old man, "two are away and they are both dead." Tinh struggled to free himself from the dream. He sat up, sweating. "No," he said aloud, "I saw them, they are both still alive." Straight away he got up, crept silently to the family shrine, and prayed. "Keep them safe, let them live. Send them back to us."

The motion of the boat awoke Hue Hue. She opened her eyes and realized that they were well out to sea. Trung was squatting next to her. Somehow he had managed to fit himself in between her and the next passenger. Drowsily she said, "Hullo, Chung Co.[34] Have you seen the others?" But before Trung could reply, Hue Hue had realized "the others" were not there. She burst into tears and her brother, weary after a night on watch, felt himself being carried away by his sister's crying.

31. **Saigon** [sī gon´]: now called Ho Chi Minh City; it was the capital of South Vietnam.
32. **Hoa** [hōä]
33. **saffron** [saf´ rən]: an orange-yellow color.
34. **Chung Co** [tyủng kō]

He, too, began to cry and they sat there, wedged one against the other in the crowd, utterly lost. After a while Trung took hold of himself. "Cheer up, Hue Hue," he said. "We'll stick together, whatever happens."

Hue Hue's eyes were fixed on the small porthole. At one moment it was filled with pale blue sky; then, as the boat rolled, the horizon came up and erased the sky until there was only blue-gray sea. Down came the horizon again until the porthole was again full of sky. Hue Hue felt very seasick. "Come on, let's go up on deck," Trung said. They managed to squeeze side by side into the row of people sitting on deck back against the boat's side, their knees gathered into their clasped hands. Hue Hue remarked to Trung: "To think there should have been forty more on board! Already we are packed like sardines."

The sun was riding up into an empty blue sky, blazing hotter every minute. Hue Hue held up her checked jacket to protect herself, but her arms soon tired and she lay down, covering her head with it. All but a few of the passengers were seasick like her. The retching and vomiting, the mess, the stench mixed with diesel fumes: Hue Hue realized that her own misery was caused not so much by the motion of the boat as by the stinking, stifling atmosphere. "Come with me, Trung," said Hue Hue, and began to make toward the bow, not walking—that was impossible—but crawling on all fours across the splayed, groaning bodies on deck. Once up in the bow, with a breeze blowing on her face, Hue Hue felt a little better. Trung too; for the first time since leaving, they exchanged a smile. It was only a fleeting one, however, for Hue Hue suddenly remembered: "This time yesterday," she said, on the verge of tears, "we were on our way to school with Quang and To."

At the other extremity of the boat, in the stern, were the heads, the latrines. There was sitting room for two on a plank placed athwartships,[35] each end supported by a beam that extended on either side just beyond the stern, so that the excrement would drop straight into the sea—a precarious perch, but at least screened from the public gaze by two half-barrels sectioned vertically.

In spite of the breeze, Trung and Hue Hue's seasickness persisted. Yet they felt hungry. Hue Hue nibbled at a *cusan*, a sweet, pulpy fruit;

35. **athwartships** [ə thwôrt′ shipz]: placed across from side to side of the ship.

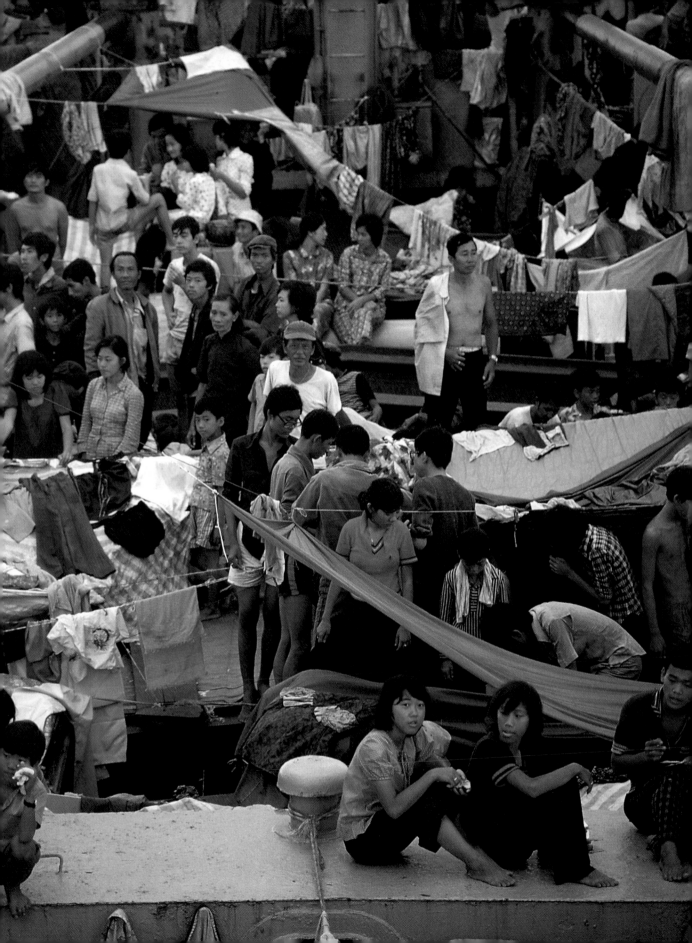

she sucked it a little and handed it to Trung, who did the same. For days, this was to be their daily portion, for the nausea and the motion of the boat made their stomachs revolt at anything more substantial. Others, recovering from their seasickness, became ravenous for solid food. They quarreled and swore at each other as they fought for their share of the rice and dried fish. Drinking water was rationed to a cup a day. It was not enough to assuage their thirst, and many of the people found some relief by jumping into the sea, a rope around them, and being trailed for a few minutes alongside. Hue Hue enjoyed this, but the salt water, as it dried out, began to eat into her striped blouse and flowered pajamas. So she remained aboard, parched from thirst, watching the waves roll past the boat and sending an occasional shower of spray over her.

When Uncle Ba was not steering, he tried to put some order into life on board, rationing the food and organizing the passengers into groups of about ten, each with a leader, and telling them to take special care of the aged and the mothers and children. Hue Hue's group included Trung, cousin Dan, and Aunt Binh. Binh was sick and depressed, and Hue Hue, too, felt so helpless with seasickness that she almost wanted to die. But Van, a girl in her twenties who was a friend of the family, urged her to hold on; it would be for only a few more days. Hue Hue was lucky with her group. Elsewhere the system broke down and it was everyone for himself.

Uncle Ba, as uncertain of his authority over the ship's company as of the direction in which it was heading, bravely tried to keep up his own and everybody else's spirits. "Don't worry," he reassured them, "last night I was navigating by the stars. We are on a steady course to Malaysia. A few more days and we shall be there." But on reaching the mouth of the River Hau Giang that morning, poor Uncle Ba had also reached the limit of his navigational experience. He had never been to sea and, on meeting it at the river's mouth, was at a complete loss. He should have altered course some 90° to the west. That would have put the boat on a course to the Malaysian coast, with a landfall somewhere near Pulau Bidong,[36] the island

36. **Pulau Bidong** [pu läw′ bē dông′]

refugee camp that had opened two months earlier, in July. Instead he swung the helm some 30° eastward and kept straight on into the middle of the most dangerous waters in Southeast Asia—the South China Sea.

The first day out, the boat began to take water, which the bilge pump spewed back into the sea. Next morning, the engine faltered, picked up, faltered again, and stopped. In a calm sea the boat hove to, and Hue Hue watched as a small group of people bent over the engine. As they tinkered with it, she heard them repeating *zoupape*, *zoupape*. She had never heard the word but it intrigued her and she asked Trung what it meant. He told her. "We borrowed it from the French, *soupape*, valve." The engine had valve trouble, a serious defect at any time but a dangerous one on the high sea, especially in a leaky boat. When the engine stopped working, the bilge pump stopped working too. The boat began to take water fast, and in the cramped space below deck men began frantically bailing, their plastic buckets full of water being passed back along a line formed by other passengers to be tipped into the sea and passed back again to the front of the line. An hour went by, then another, as the powerless boat drifted. During that time two merchantmen passed not more than a half mile away and the people on the roof of the wheelhouse waved energetically. Their efforts were in vain; without a sign of recognition, the big ships sailed on their way, while the boat people hurled insults and curses after them, not believing that their signals could be so flagrantly ignored. Nothing that had happened so far had so demoralized them. They felt better when they heard the engine splutter once more into life; a thin cheer went up, and the boat was again under way, making about three miles an hour.

The second day out from land was ending; by now, the passengers, though they did not realize it, had almost crossed the main shipping lanes and were heading for an empty desert of water. Since the engine failure they had passed one more merchantman, but Ba had warned: "Don't make any sign. It looks like a Soviet ship." The

Russians were known to pick up boat people and land them back in Vietnam, a fate worse than drowning.

That night the engine stopped twice more, and each time pandemonium broke out below, with the fetid air full of cries and swearwords—"Fix the engine, for God's sake; we're going to sink"—and the screaming of frightened children. Flashlights shone and buckets were again passed from hand to hand. A gale began blowing up—it was the tail of the monsoon[37] season—and the helpless, overloaded boat, tossed here and there by the waves, took so much water that it felt as if it were going to capsize. Then the motor started up, the boat moved forward again, and the panic subsided.

All next day the gale blew and torrents of rain, cold and stinging, blotted out the horizon. The engine kept breaking down; each time it did so, the boat people bailed for their lives. On deck, the people at the end of the line, lashed by the rain, cold, drenched, and exhausted, began to protest. In vain Ba encouraged them: "Come on, stick to it, keep bailing or we're lost." They answered: "Nothing doing. The boat's going to sink anyway!" Others took their place. For another day and night the boat people fought the storms and the faulty engine and somehow kept their craft afloat.

At last the big seas subsided into long, heaving swells and flying fish scudded across the rolling purple-blue valleys of water. No spray flew and the sea no longer came pouring over the gunwales. A fiery sun sailed again into the sky and dried out the deck till it was warm. But the problem of the engine remained; bailing had become a routine operation. On the eighth day of the voyage, the sea became still and flat; not a breath of wind rippled its glassy surface. The engine seemed to catch the mood; though it still ran unevenly, sending vibrations through the length of the boat, it miraculously kept going. By evening huge, bulbing cumulus clouds had ballooned up high into the sky, reflecting and diffusing the last rays of the setting sun and forming an unbroken barrage whose lower surface almost touched the horizon.

37. **monsoon** [mon sün′]: the rainy season during which the wind of the same name blows from the southwest.

In the fading, pink-gold light the boat chugged on, throwing up a little phosphorescent bow wave that slid down each side until its dancing sparks were extinguished in the turbulence of the wake.

With Trung beside her, Hue Hue had been watching the sunset. Her thoughts temporarily distracted by its splendor, she forgot her pangs of hunger and the nausea that had cloyed her throat and the pit of her stomach for over a week. Life had dragged on painfully through long, anxious days and restless nights—days and nights punctuated by periods of stifling heat; by raging storms and the anguished cries of frightened people; by the frequent failures of an old and unreliable engine, whose pungent fumes mingled with the stench of sick humanity; and, at last, by the calm that had fallen over the sea and the boat itself.

Throughout the turmoil of the voyage, Hue Hue's thoughts had dwelt ceaselessly on her parents and brothers back in Vietnam. She was only thirteen; she missed her family terribly and cried whenever she imagined them at home. But Binh and Van had been sweet to her; Trung was always at her side; and Dan helped to encourage her.

She looked around the crowded deck. Where were they going, all these people, most of them unknown to her? Before them lay nothing but sea, stretching out to the horizon, and the clouds, now darkening into gray against a vivid blue-green sky.

It began to get chilly, so Hue Hue and Trung moved below, squeezed themselves in between some others, and sat down with their backs against the ship's side. As the day died so did the sound of garrulous voices. People were chatting quietly now, and peace and order had returned to the boat. Hue Hue and Trung began to doze.

Suddenly a harsh, grating sound and the crash of splitting timber jolted everyone into wakefulness. The boat came to an abrupt standstill. Through the broken hull water gushed past their feet and people shouted: "We're aground—everybody up on deck!" From their cramped quarters below, there followed a rush of old men and women, of mothers clasping their children to them or dragging them by the hand. The young men and girls clambered up last. Everyone on deck was talking excitedly. "We have hit land all right, but where? Malaysia? Thailand?" No one could answer, least of all Uncle Ba. Then above the hubbub came a voice, and a young man pointed into the fading light: "Look, a ship! There! A ship at anchor!" People peered after him and cried: "Yes, it's a ship! We're saved!" Some shook hands and embraced; others were too weary for joy.

Few of them slept that night, partly through excitement, partly because they had to camp as best they could on deck. The boat was filling fast, until, around midnight, the water, a yard deep inside the hull, had risen to the level of the sea outside. At least that would keep the boat on an even keel.

To Hue Hue the boat now felt as solid as a house. Her sickness disappeared, but like everybody else, she could not sleep. She lay there on the hard deck in the dark, her cardigan over her, a frightened little girl marooned somewhere in the middle of the sea.

PETER TOWNSEND

Peter Townsend was born in 1914 in Rangoon, Burma where his father, an Englishman, served in the Indian army. Townsend went to school and college in England. Royal Air Force College prepared him for a lifetime career. Townsend served first in Singapore, and then as a fighter pilot during the Battle of Britain in 1939-1941. After World War II, he was assigned to the Royal household as personal attendant first to King George VI and then to Queen Elizabeth II. When he retired in 1956, Townsend became a full-time author and journalist.

Townsend wrote an outstanding history of the Battle of Britain, called *Duel of Eagles*. The book includes his own memories as well as those of some German pilots whom he interviewed. Probably his most valuable books are the stories of children in war and what it can do to them. Townsend has said that he was always "impressed by children's dignity, their longing for revenge, sometimes their forgiveness." He intends these stories to be a record so that no one will forget these children, Townsend has said. "I am their witness." Among these books is *The Girl in the White Ship*.

Mother to Son

Langston Hughes

Stairs, Provincetown Charles Demuth, 1920, gouache and pencil on cardboard, 23$\frac{1}{2}$" x 19$\frac{1}{2}$", The Museum of Modern Art, New York

Well, son, I'll tell you:
Life for me ain't been no crystal stair.
It's had tacks in it,
And splinters,
And boards torn up,   5
And places with no carpet on the floor—
Bare.
But all the time
I'se been a-climbin' on,
And reachin' landin's,   10
And turnin' corners,
And sometimes goin' in the dark
Where there ain't been no light.
So boy, don't you turn back.
Don't you set down on the steps   15
'Cause you finds it's kinder hard.
Don't you fall now
For I'se still goin', honey,
I'se still climbin',
And life for me ain't been no crystal stair.   20

LANGSTON HUGHES

James Langston Hughes [1902-1967] was born in Joplin, Missouri. In 1926, Hughes published his first book of poems, titled *The Weary Blues*. His work was widely praised and won him a college scholarship to Lincoln University in Pennsylvania. Hughes graduated in 1929 just as the Depression began. He had to make a living writing, as he said, to "turn poetry into bread. It was a question of writing or starving." His work was "largely concerned with the depicting of Negro life in America." To accomplish this, he used rhythm, dialect, and the sounds of the Harlem streets. Besides poetry, Hughes wrote short stories, novels, essays, movie scripts, and plays.

I'd Like to Go Alone Nina Ledererová, drawing in pencil and watercolor, State Jewish Museum, Prague, the Czech Republic

SONIA SCHREIBER WEITZ

from

I *promised* I *would tell*

A s you will read in the following selection, Sonia Schreiber and her family were forced by the Nazis[1] to leave their home and move into a crowded, walled ghetto[2] with other Polish Jews. While Sonia lived in a room with her parents and three other families, Sonia's older sister Blanca and Blanca's husband Norbert belonged for a time to the Polish underground[3] and were able to help the family get food and other necessities.

1. **Nazis** [nä′ tsēz]: members of the National Socialist Party in Germany, led by Aldolf Hitler.
2. **ghetto** [get′ ō]: section of a city where Jews were forced to live.
3. **underground:** movement in which people worked in secret against the Nazis.

I was twelve and a half in March 1941 when my family was forced into the ghetto. I remained there for two years. During those years, I recorded my thoughts in a diary. I had always liked to write, and in the ghetto I found that writing helped me cope a little better with the horrors around me. I especially liked writing poetry, so I also included poems in my diary.

Although my diary did not survive the war, the memory of what I had experienced and written in the ghetto did not fade. So in 1946, one year after the war ended, I sat down to write about my life in the ghetto. In fact, I tried to reconstruct from memory the original pages of my diary. The following pages contain an English translation of the "reconstructed diary" which I wrote in 1946. (In some cases, I have edited the original manuscript for clarity.)

April 1941

A month after entering the ghetto, orders came that I had to go to work. One day, other young people and I were piled into a truck and taken out of the ghetto to scrub latrines in the German barracks. At night, as we returned to the ghetto, the soldiers forced us to sing "Roll Out the Barrel" for their amusement. They laughed at the humiliation we faced in singing a cheerful tune after a day of cleaning up their filth. They also laughed because we sang in Polish, a language that the Germans considered inferior.

My mother cried that I had to do this work; she cried bitterly, although she tried to hide it. My father smoked one cigarette after the other. He looked at me with love and pity. He quietly whispered, "That's war. That's the horrible war." I think he felt guilty. The poor man knew that, even in the ghetto, if you had extra money or something of value, it was often possible to find a strong person to work in the place of a child. And so if he had the money, perhaps he could have found a substitute laborer for his beloved little girl. But we barely had money to buy food and no more valuables left. I could see the helplessness in his eyes as I went off to work.

November 1941

One evening, I returned hungry and tired to the house to see my father at the door. He seemed very worried and looked very pale. He asked me to be quiet because my mother was sick. "Sick? How could that be?" I asked. I had never seen my mother sick. No matter how tired or weak, she would always smile, hug me, and say that everything would be all right, that things would get better, that we would be going home soon, that Friday night there would be candles on the white tablecloth again, and that all would be well.

Without making a sound, I tiptoed into the dark room. She was asleep. I lit the small light and came nearer. Her face was burning and her eyes were cloudy. *Mamusiu*,[4] I whispered. I kneeled by her bed and touched her forehead. She gazed at me with a distant look. "My God, she does not know me," I thought. "Her own daughter, and she does not know me."

Later that night, she was taken to the ghetto hospital. She was very sick, suffering from meningitis.[5] Since the hospital was a place for the contagiously ill, none of us were allowed to visit her. But somehow Blanca managed to get extra food and smuggle it in to my mother. My father and I paced endlessly in front of the hospital. Weeks passed in constant fear that the hospital might be evacuated or that the patients might be executed before my mother recovered.

Finally, one day, wrapped in a blanket, my mother came to the window and waved to us. Oh, how good it was to see her! Soon after, she came home, pale and weak. Blanca continued scrounging and somehow was always able to find extra food for our mother.

March 1942

By the spring of 1942 we had almost no money left. So one day I took the last of our money and went to the bakery for bread. I looked at length at the wonderfully fresh pungent loaves of bread. I faced the

---

4. **Mamusiu** [mä mǔʹ sù]: (also *mamusia*) Polish for "Mama."
5. **meningitis** [men ʹ in jīʹ tis]: an illness that is often fatal.

baker and breathlessly blurted out a long rehearsed question, "Would you trust me with ten loaves of bread at nine *zloty*[6] each, and I will bring the money tomorrow morning?" The answer came quickly, "Fine."

I could not believe it. I was so proud of myself. I took the ten loaves of bread and ran from one building to another, from one apartment to another, selling each loaf for ten *zloty*. Simple math. Each day I would earn enough money to buy a loaf of bread for my family.

On the evening of the first day, I hid the money under my pillow to protect it until morning. When morning came, I rushed to the bakery and purchased the bread. Slightly embarrassed but happy, I presented the bread to my utterly amazed mother. Unfortunately, this enterprise did not last. Orders came from the Germans to shut down the ghetto bakeries.

Still, we had to have money. So *mamusia* came up with the following plan. In the back of the house in which we lived, there was a garden—once beautiful but now brown and overgrown with weeds. In that little backyard, *mamusia* created a nursery for those children whose lives had been temporarily spared but whose parents were forced into slave labor each day. Many of these parents gladly paid whatever they could to place their children in our care.

It would still be dark when I would get up in the morning and rush from one ghetto house to another, collecting the sleepy-eyed youngsters to bring to our backyard. While my mother cooked and did the laundry, I amused the children with their favorite fairy tales. My imagination was inexhaustible, and in the sunlight I watched their happy smiling faces full of wonderment and hope.

Often, while the children napped, I would sit in the shade of a tree in that dead garden. Enjoying the few precious moments of quiet, I would fill the pages of my diary with my thoughts and feelings. I wrote that I desperately wanted to be good and kind and helpful to my *mamusia*. I wrote also about life—how precious it was and how much I wanted the horrible war to come to an end. In my childish handwriting, I wrote prayers, pleading with God for help. Somehow,

6. *zloty* [slō′ tē]

Girl with Star Leo Haas, 1943, pen and ink wash on paper, 16 ¹/₂″ x 9⁷/₈″, State Jewish Museum, Prague, the Czech Republic

I believed He would hear my prayers and answer them. I trusted that the future would be better. In the blessed quiet of these moments, I also wrote poetry.

A Quiet Time

. . . a peaceful moment
to heal my soul
to steady the pounding
within my breast
. . . a quiet time
to make me whole
and let me rest

June 1942

One day in June of our second year in the ghetto, my mother got sick again. This time she refused to go to the hospital. She did not want to waste any time being separated from us. I guess she knew that our time together could be cut short any day. Transports[7] of the old, the sick, and the young were constantly leaving, never to be heard from again.

Each day my father and I carried a cot outdoors for my mother. There, in the shade of my tree, she seemed most comfortable. Often, my father would watch her from afar. He seemed so sad and embarrassed by his helplessness. My heart ached for him, but I knew that I could not approach him and discuss his feelings. He was perhaps more pitiful and bewildered than the rest of us.

Slowly, my mother returned to health. Again, to me, our little nest seemed secure. I began to study in an "underground" school where I met other young people. Education was, of course, forbidden in the ghetto, but there was a group of dedicated Jewish teachers who designed lesson plans for us, giving our young lives a degree of order and defiance.

My new school friends invited me to a "picnic" and I learned to dance. I went for long walks with my friend Rena,[8] who was in love with Bubek,[9] while I was crazy about Jerzyk.[10] Rena and I understood each other. We were both teenagers, after all.

My parents also insisted that I learn to do something useful. So I became apprenticed to a seamstress. This skill helped me get a job in a German factory called Madrich.[11] Since as a seamstress I was useful to the Germans, I was able to avoid early deportation.

We had a very active resistance movement in the ghetto. As a matter of fact, many of my friends were part of the movement. At one point, I was going to leave the ghetto and join the underground

---

7. **Transports:** in this context, the moving of people to a place where they were killed.
8. **Rena** [re′ nä]
9. **Bubek** [bü′ beg]
10. **Jerzyk** [yer′ sēg]
11. **Madrich** [mä′ drikH]

to fight against the Nazis. But, since the Polish partisans[12] rarely accepted Jewish men and women into their units, Jewish resistance fighters faced a tremendous obstacle. We had to change our appearances so that we looked Polish.

My pug nose, which I had always hated so much, was in my favor. But, since most Polish people had fair skin and light hair coloring, my dark hair was a problem. So my mother dyed my hair blond. Then, somehow, she and my father managed to get me the necessary false papers, and I was ready to go.

Unfortunately, the group of youngsters which left just before me was denounced by Poles who collaborated with the Nazis. The Poles turned them in to the Gestapo for the meager reward of a bag of sugar. The Gestapo shot them, one and all. When my parents heard about this act of outrage, they decided that I was to remain in the ghetto.

Still, not all of the Polish people turned against us. For example, the members of one Polish family risked their lives to hide Jadzia,[13] Norbert's niece. As a result of their courage, Jadzia survived the war.

In the meantime, life in the ghetto became "hot." The lists for "resettlement"[14] were growing longer and longer. Without our knowing it, we were condemned to death, but first the Nazis subjected us to unbearable physical and mental tortures.

October 1942

Inevitably, summer turned into fall. By this time, the school we ran was no longer in business. The Nazis had taken all of our children for resettlement. One day in October, I was sitting under my tree writing, when I heard my mother's voice. "Sonia! *Sloneczko!*"[15] (She often called me "Sunshine.") In the window, I could see her silhouette. "Come in, child. It is getting cold outside."

---

12. **partisans** [pär′ tə zenz]: members of the underground.
13. **Jadzia** [yäd′ zä]
14. **resettlement:** in this context, the moving of people to another place in order to kill them.
15. *Sloneczko* [slō nech′ gō]

For a moment, I stood at the door and gazed at the dirty blanket that separated one family from another. Then my gaze shifted to my mother. I looked at her as if I were seeing her for the first time. What I saw filled me with shock and surprise. Apparently I had not looked at her closely for a long time. All at once I realized that her hair had turned gray. There were teeth missing in her smile. Her hands were chapped and raw, and her eyes were very, very sad.

That evening, I sat by the window for a long time watching the blood-red sunset. The stars glimmered like pure gold. The moon rose mocking my dreams and hopes. I closed my eyes remembering my childhood through tears. It seemed like a hundred years ago that I had gone to school, played with other children, and looked forward to springtime. How good my life had been. Yet even then, there had been signs of danger all around me. And so I wrote:

How Could We Know

How could we know

What danger signs foretell

We watched the clouds

And heard the thunder near

Until the lightning struck

And darkness fell

But that was yesteryear

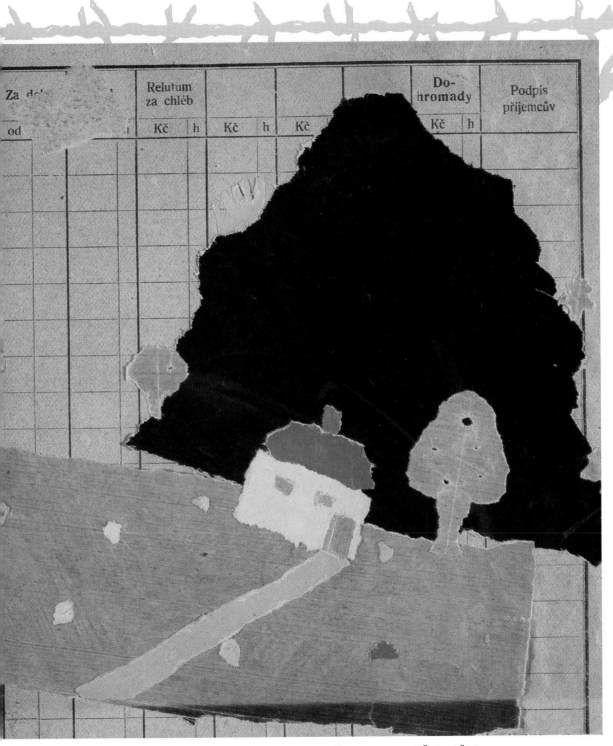

Home in Landscape Eva Brandeis, 1944, collage on paper, 7⁷/₈" x 9⁷/₈",
State Jewish Museum, Prague, the Czech Republic

I was deep in thought about the past and fantasizing about the future when I sensed my mother's hand stroking my hair. By now the room was very cold. We got into bed to keep each other warm. We rested quietly for a long time in this dark dingy room. There was no need for words. I knew that my mother loved me more than her very life. Of course, she loved Blanca as much. She loved Norbert too as if he were her own son. But Blanca and Norbert had each other. And me? In her eyes I was still a child, and she worried desperately about what would happen to me.

Admittedly, I was just an average daughter. I am sure that I could have done many things better. I could have listened more closely. I could have behaved more like a lady. But I did love her deeply. I realized that night what the word "mother" meant to me.

Late that night we were awakened by my father's footsteps. He was very upset. He uttered only two words, "Another transport." I sat up in bed half asleep and looked at him. "Who are they taking this time?" I asked. "Lie down, child," my mother's voice was incredibly calm. "It is God's will."

I cuddled up next to her. We were warm and comfortable. I could feel her heart beating. I held on to her with all my strength. I wanted to feel her next to me. I needed the closeness. I wanted her all to myself. I was afraid that this might be our last embrace, our final chance to be close. I did not dare move. But my eyes were wide open, staring at the dirty gray ceiling. Her arm was across my chest, and I listened to her short uneven breaths.

We waited. Each moment seemed like an eternity. Somewhere a clock struck twelve midnight. Suddenly there were heavy footsteps, and we heard the dreaded pounding on the door. Two men in uniform forced the door open and entered the room. "Adela Schreiber," one voice said. "Get dressed! Immediately!" I froze. My mother sat up on the edge of the bed and slowly started putting on her stockings and her shoes. She put a scarf on her head. "Dress warmly," the voice continued. "You are going on a long journey!"

I ran out into the yard. I screamed into the night, but no sound came from my lips. The sounds were in my head. I thought I would go mad with grief and rage. I stood there like a stone looking at the sky, cursing the heavens in silence. In reality, the night was quite calm and beautiful. Just an October night in the year 1942. How was it possible that the sky was so peaceful, and where was God?

Suddenly, I found my voice. I cried out, "God, Oh God, Help! How can You let this happen? How can You not be touched by this child whose mother is being taken away by force?"

I trembled as I walked back into the house. I heard doors open and shut and footsteps in the street. "Sonia, Sonia." Now it was my father's voice that pierced the night. "Your mother fainted, and the police have left. For the moment, they are gone. But they will return with a stretcher."

I came into the room. My mother was lying on the floor. Although she had fainted, her eyes were now wide open. Absent-mindedly, she was smoothing out her hair. I heard my father cry, "Oh child, oh child." I came up to him. He was weeping. Something inside of me died. I too wanted to cry but could not. I wanted to speak, to comfort him. I wanted to . . . I do not know what I wanted.

By now, my mother had stood up. Once again, she began getting dressed. Slowly, deliberately, she put on her dress, her sweater, a coat. How carefully she dressed. Calmly and with great care, as if she were getting ready to go to a cinema, she combed her hair. Then she took a bag from the closet. From the cupboard, she took a piece of dry bread and put it into the bag. Dry bread, how terrible! All the time, I stood there, watching her in horror.

Suddenly the door opened, and two men came in with a stretcher. "Where is the sick person?" they asked. Their eyes quickly located my mother. They motioned to the stretcher. "Get on quickly so we can go!" "No, thank you," said my mother in a strange, distant voice. "I am going to make it on my own. No need for the stretcher." Then she added with dignity, "I can walk."

She turned to me. "Come closer, *Sloneczko*," she whispered. I obeyed. She took something from her bag, some money. She put it into my hand. "I know you will need this. It may help." She put her arms around me and whispered, "Remember, I love you." The world was spinning in front of my eyes. As if from afar I heard her last words, "And remember to tell the world!"

"Put an end to this sentimental crap. Enough! Let's go!" yelled the harsh voices. "No, stop, I am going with you," said my father. He went with them, and suddenly I was alone in the night.

Again I called on God for help. I screamed out to the deaf heartless world. Then, exhausted, I dozed in agony and dreams until I heard my father's voice. "Sonia, child, we saved your mother. Somehow Blanca found out that *mamusia* was on the list. She knew the police must pass by her house on their way to the roundup in the square. So she watched for your mother. Blanca, Norbert, and I managed to create some confusion—a diversion that momentarily caused the police to let go of her. In that split second, we grabbed *mamusia* and hid her in a nearby shed. Then I made a deal with the police. I told them I would go in her place."

I gasped. "Oh, that is nothing," continued my father. "I am a man, and I am strong. I will be fine. The important thing is that your mother is safe." "Safe?" I must be dreaming. "Who said that? It could not be." But my father was standing over me. Suddenly I jumped up and faced him. "No, you are not going! You will not keep your word to the police!"

My father looked at me in bewilderment. I shook him. "Listen! You are not going. Rena's father has connections. He will help later when the *akcja*[16] is over. He will get us whatever papers we need. In the meantime, we will hide together with *mamusia*."

We both rushed to the courtyard. Blanca and Norbert had already been forced to join their work detail. I ran around in panic, looking for Rena's father. When I finally found him, he said that we had done the smart thing. He advised us to hide together. Then, if we survived this *akcja*, he would somehow manage to get us the proper "life" permits.

I hurried back to the courtyard where I saw many members of Norbert's family whispering with my father. The look in my father's

16. *akcja* [äg′ tzyä]

eyes told me that there was trouble. "We cannot hide with *mamusia* in the shed," he said. His eyes filled with tears. "The shed is locked, and we cannot find the key." We looked at each other in horror. By now the SS men—those in charge of resettlements and killing—were chasing people to the gathering place, or *Appelplatz*.[17] Their voices taunted us. "*Heraus!*[18] *Heraus!* Get out, you bastards! This is resettlement. Get out of hiding, you lousy Jews! Get out! Get out!"

The voices were dangerously near. We could not break open the shed door without attracting attention. I sneaked up to the door and whispered, "*Mamusiu*, it's me, Sonia. We cannot open the door. There are too many Germans around. We are going to hide nearby in a cellar. Can you hear me?" "Oh, I would like to be with you," she answered. "We'll be together soon," I promised.

Suddenly I heard shots. There were screams too. My father forced me to move. In the distance, I heard my mother's muffled voice, "Yes, yes, good. Take care of yourself. . ." and the words faded.

We jumped into a basement—my father and I and some other people. We soon realized that Norbert's family was hiding in a cellar next to us. It was dark and damp. Groping, we found some old furniture, and we barricaded the doors and windows. Slowly my eyes became adjusted to the darkness. My father took some crumbs of bread out of his pocket and gave them to me. I ate. I cuddled up next to him. With horror, I listened to the sounds coming from the street. Gunfire . . . One shot after another . . . Terrifying screams, and then quiet and the sound of heavy boots. The blood-curdling screams of children. Those screams surely reached the heavens . . . or did they?

Hours went by. Night passed, and the sun was shining again. We did not respond to the voices from the loudspeakers outside—voices that assured us that we best come out . . . that we would be taken to work . . . that there would be plenty of food and good living conditions. But the voices also warned us that if we did not come out but continued to hide, we would be killed on the spot when they found us.

17. *Appelplatz* [ä pel′ pläts]
18. *Heraus* [här ouz′]

At some point, I heard a voice, quiet and calm, calling my name. The voice sounded like that of Cyla,[19] Norbert's sister. My father and I looked at each other. "Let's go," I said. "Quiet, we are not going," whispered my father, putting his hand on my mouth.

Again we heard cries and screams. Through the crack in the window, I saw feet, thousands of feet. Some were clad in boots; some in once-elegant high-heeled shoes. Some were marching; others stumbled. Then I saw a tiny foot, a child's foot, tripping on a stone. The little girl, perhaps four years old, cried out as she fell. The next thing I heard was a gunshot. The crying stopped. And then there were more shoes, big and small, in a last silent march before death.

The sun was setting once more. We sensed a terrifying silence, and this time the silence lasted. My father said, "I think it is safe to go out. Let us go and look for your mother." I got up. I was completely paralyzed. My body would not respond, would not move. My father helped me crawl out onto the courtyard. Immediately, we headed for the shed.

By now, I was so numb that the scene before me did not penetrate my consciousness. It was too horrible to confront. The doors to the shed had been ripped open by an ax or a rifle butt. My mother was gone. On the floor lay a crumpled blanket.

My heart sank. If only we had found her body in the shed. If only she had been killed immediately and spared any further suffering. "Oh God, how I wish she had been killed right here. Then I could throw my arms around her and . . . but now there is nothing but emptiness in the shed and in my soul." That night, I wrote:

19. **Cyla** [tzē′ lä]

Sonia's mother, Adela Finder Schreiber

In Memory to My Mother

Where is your grave?
Where did you die?
Why did you go away?
Why did you leave
Your little girl   5
That rainy autumn day?

I still can hear
The words you spoke:
"You tell the world, my child."
Your eyes as green   10
as emeralds
Were quiet and so mild.

You held my hand
Your face was white
And silent like a stone,   15
You pressed something
Into my palm . . .
And then . . . then you were gone.

I *suffered, but*
I *didn't cry:*   20
The pain so fierce, so deep . . .
It pierced my heart
And squeezed it dry . . .
And then, I fell asleep.

Asleep in agony   25
And dreams . . .
A nightmare that was true . . .
I heard the shots,
The screams that came
From us, from me and you.   30

I promised I would
Tell the world . . .
But where to find the words
To speak of
Innocence and love,   35
And tell how much it hurts . . .

About those faces
Weak and pale,
Those dizzy eyes around,
And countless lips   40
That whispered "help"
But never made a sound . . .

To tell about
The loss . . . the grief,
The dread of death and cold,   45
Of wickedness
And misery . . .
O no! . . . it can't be told.

Later, the rumors we had been hearing and our worst fears were confirmed, mostly by the underground. I learned that my beautiful mother had been taken to the death camp Belzec.[20] I never saw her again.

My mother's disappearance made me feel old, terribly old. Some people tried to comfort me. Others told me to stop crying, to stop acting like a child. But I could not stop grieving. I remembered how my mother had grieved when her mother had been killed.[21] And so I yelled back that it is right to cry when you lose your *mamusia*. My mother was not a child when her mother was killed. Yet she too cried. Now, like her, I was grown up, and I too could cry if I wanted to.

20. **Belzec** [bel′ sek]
21. **when her mother had been killed:** Sonia's grandmother was killed by the Nazis in 1940.

Sonia's grandmother with her children. Sonia's mother is in front.

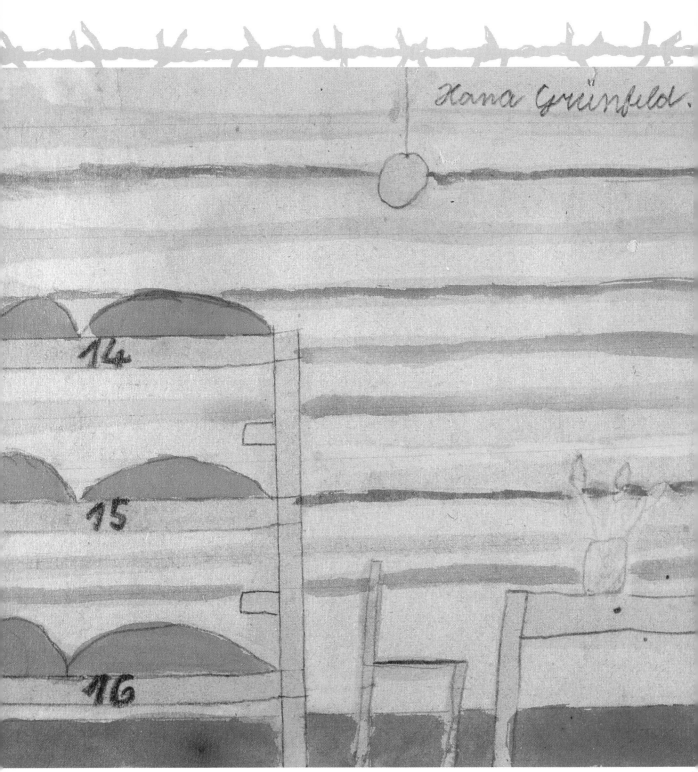

Drawing Kana Grünfeld, drawing in pencil and watercolor,
State Jewish Museum, Prague, the Czech Republic

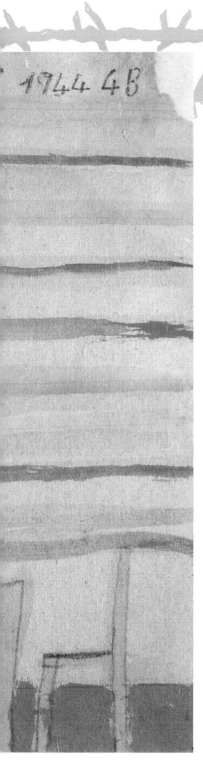

1944 48

Sonia and Blanca went from the ghetto to a succession of five concentration camps. In May 1945, they were finally freed by American troops. The sisters, together with Blanca's husband Norbert, came to the United States.

SONIA SCHREIBER WEITZ

Sonia Schreiber Weitz was born in 1928 in Kraków, Poland, and had a happy childhood until Germany took over Poland. While living in the ghetto and in concentration camps, she wrote poetry to help her cope with the fear and suffering all around her. Weitz says that she owes her life to her sister Blanca who made certain that they were never separated while they were in concentration camps.

After World War II, Blanca and Sonia were reunited with Blanca's husband Norbert in Austria. They remained displaced persons until 1948 when Norbert's uncle in Massachusetts sent for them to come to the United States.

Two years later, Sonia Schreiber married and eventually had a son and twin daughters. Her loving family and her own writing helped her to come to terms with her past. In recent years, Weitz has been active in teaching people about the Holocaust. She also trains other teachers, speaks publicly about her experiences, and continues to write poetry.

from *I Promised I Would Tell* **59**

We Shall Wait Forever

▲▲▲▲

Darlene Sinyella

*B*ack in the past
we, the ancestors, ruled the
quiet lands.
We would sit around camp fires
and sing with harmony.   5
The beating of the drums sounded
like the heart of an Indian. The cry
of a wolf, the howl of an owl, put us
into the secrets of ourselves.
Then we woke in the early mist of May,   10
and found ourselves in front
of our enemies, who had come to fight.
The children cried, the women ran
and hid. The men who were brave
stood up for us.   15
We fought, but many of us died.
Our spirits now haunt
the lands we walked on.
Now we sing, laugh, dance, and lie
under the bright blue sky. We are waiting 20
for our enemies who killed us to pass by.
We shall stay here and wait until
we find them. Until then we shall wait
in peace and harmony.

DARLENE SINYELLA

Darlene Sinyella, who is a Native American of the Hualapai Nation, wrote "We Shall Wait Forever" when she was in the seventh grade at the Hualapai Elementary School in Peach Springs, Arizona. Her poem was published in 1990 in an anthology of Native American student poetry titled *A Tree Full of Leaves Which Are Stars*.

HOLDING OUT

OUIDA SEBESTYEN

CHARACTERS

CURTIS
VALERIE
INDIANS OF THE MODOC[1] TRIBE

SETTING

TIME: *The present, late afternoon on a chilly spring day.*

A roadside rest area. One sturdy picnic table with benches and a trash can are the only signs of civilization. Behind them, in dimmer light, jagged outcroppings of lava rock and clumps of sagebrush stair-step up a desolate slope. A drum is beating softly, almost like the thump of a heart.

AT CURTAIN RISE: CURTIS *strides out among the rocks at right. He is sixteen, and comfortable being alone. He stumbles on a stone and pushes it out of the trail with a slender branch he is using as a staff. He also carries the thin National Park Service booklet he has used on a self-guided hike. He looks around and, because no one is there to see, holds it with his teeth so he can pretend his staff is a rifle. After a few quick shots he climbs up on the table and continues to read, deeply interested. A truck door slams. He stiffens. A few moments later* VALERIE *appears, dressed like him in jeans and sweatshirt, raking her tangled hair. Neither of them takes notice of the drum, which slowly fades away.*

1. **Modoc** [mō′ dok]: Native American people from southern Oregon and northern California.

VALERIE: Curtis, don't *do* stuff like this to me. I woke up and there I was, parked all by myself in the middle of nowhere, with my feet out the window.

CURTIS (*pointing up the slope*): There's a trail up there that makes a loop. So I walked around it, to get the kinks out.

VALERIE: Yeah, tell me about kinks. I feel like the Hunchback of Notre Dame. How long did I sleep?

CURTIS: About six hours.

VALERIE: You're kidding. Nobody can sleep six hours in the cab of a pickup truck and live to tell about it.

CURTIS: Well, I guess you just made medical history.

VALERIE: Where *is* this? Are we still in Oregon?

CURTIS (*taking a pebble out of his shoe*): No, we've crossed back into California. After you didn't wake up, I thought, What am I supposed to be doing? So I pulled off the highway and stopped here.

VALERIE: Oh, man—no. Not back in California.

CURTIS: What was I supposed to do, with you zonked out? Turn west and drive till we went down in the Pacific, blub, blub, blub?

VALERIE: You could have waked me up, for starters.

CURTIS (*softening*): I guess. But you'd done nearly all the driving last night, and you looked really pooped. Snoring away like that. I sort of—

VALERIE: I wasn't tired from last night. I was tired from this morning.

CURTIS: Yeah, I know. I saw it. When you came out of your dad's house, you looked really different. Your face was white. I thought maybe he'd hit you, or something, and that's why you wouldn't say anything when I tried to talk.

VALERIE: No, I just had to—I don't know—get into a little dark space and stay really quiet for a while. Curled up. Like a snail. And just wait till the shock wore off. Okay?

CURTIS: Hey, you don't have to explain it. I just didn't know what to do. So I just kept on driving and thinking and wondering. One spot up there in the mountains I was screaming along through this snowstorm. In my dad's truck. Oh, man. I never drove in a snowstorm before. So I thought I better stop, for Pete's sake, and hang around here till you joined the world again.

VALERIE (*looking around*): You didn't pick a really great spot, Curt. This is pretty awful.

CURTIS: I don't know—it's kind of interesting. All this dark-red jagged rock is hardened lava. You know, like Hawaii.

VALERIE: It figures: I go to sleep in a truck and wake up in a lava bed. Couldn't you have stopped in a town? What am I supposed to do for a rest room?

CURTIS: There's one up the trail. Over past that dark bunch of junipers.

VALERIE: Oh, great. It would be. (*She takes a few uncertain steps that bring her back to her starting point.*) Did you read the same thing I did about some kidnaper or hired killer or somebody—

CURTIS: Oh, that? Yeah—he dumped the body in one of these pits. Not out in the bushes where nobody ever goes—no, it's got to be in there where some Park Service guy can notice it. But I guess maybe he was thinking the quicklime[2] or whatever would dissolve the—

VALERIE: Curtis! Shut up. Just shut up—you're gross. I'm not in any shape for scary stories. Or this weirdo place, whatever it is.

CURTIS: It's a national monument. So don't put it down—the government's trying hard to keep weirdo places like this unspoiled for our grandchildren. (*He rethinks.*) Well, not *our* grandchildren . . .

VALERIE: So where is everybody?

CURTIS: I guess March is still off season. There's maybe some kind of visitors' center, farther up the road. But it's probably closed. So people just drive through, like us.

VALERIE: No store, or anything? What do we eat?

2. **quicklime:** calcium oxide, a water-soluble solid; in this context, it would destroy a body.

CURTIS: We've still got the apples. And potato chips. I can go see what else.

VALERIE (*uneasily*)**:** Okay. And I guess I can go see if anybody is stashed in the outhouse. (*She starts off again, and turns back.*) Curtis, if I yell, you better come running.

CURTIS: Don't I always? (*His question stops her, and they lock eyes. She jerks around and goes up left among the looming lava shapes. He goes off to the parked truck.*)

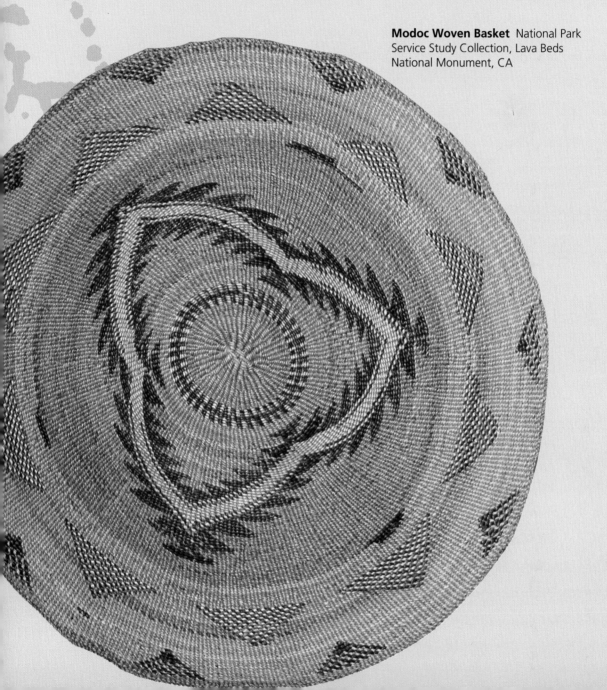

Modoc Woven Basket National Park Service Study Collection, Lava Beds National Monument, CA

A MODOC INDIAN SENTRY *stands up unhurriedly from behind a rock and watches them go. Another* SENTRY *rises from his nearby hiding place. They wear simple rough shirts and pants, and round flat-brimmed hats decorated with feathers. Their faces and hands, their clothing and moccasins, their cartridge belts and long 1870's rifles, are shades of gray, as if they were being seen through gauze, or the haze of time. They study the horizon carefully, pointing and nodding to each other. Their movements are slow, almost trancelike with fatigue. They watch with quiet interest as* CURTIS *returns and puts two paper sacks and a can of pop on the table. His gaze goes past them and he starts to read.* VALERIE *comes back and walks past them, unaware.*

VALERIE: Yuck. Can't they design those things to flush or something? (*She is holding a large feather, which she sticks into her hair.*) Boy, talk about primitive.

CURTIS: Beats a bush.

VALERIE: Just barely.

CURTIS (*noticing the feather*): What's that?

VALERIE: I found it. Some critter got ambushed, I reckon. Oh, great, you found something to drink.

CURTIS: If you don't mind drinking from the same can.

VALERIE: You're really cute, Curt. Here we are, runaways, with a practically stolen truck on our hands, and maybe the police hunting us by now. And your folks yelling, "Where's our baby boy!" And my mom blaming everybody in sight—and you make it sound like we're on a shy little first date. (*She drinks and hands him the can.*) Hey, you found the cookies. I forgot we saved some. (*She divvies them up.*) I'm starved! Aren't you?

CURTIS (*gently nudging her toward reality*): Valerie, this is all the food we've got. And we're running low on gas. We need to talk about what we're doing.

VALERIE: We know what we're doing. We're having a picnic in lava land. (*She starts to eat an apple from one of the sacks.*)

CURTIS: No, what we're doing is putting off talking about what happened. And what we're going to do *now*. What direction we're going.

VALERIE: Curtis, give me a break. I'm not ready. It's too soon—it's just too—Eat. Okay?

CURTIS (*regretfully*): Val, your dad doesn't want you. You've got to go back home.

VALERIE: Back home? What home? (*She forces an airy laugh.*) You mean my mom's apartment, where I hang my clothes and step over the bottles? That home?

CURTIS: Whatever you call it, it's the only place you've got to live in.

VALERIE: That's a big lie. I've got the whole world to live in. I can live right here. People live in trucks.

CURTIS: Not in my dad's truck, they don't.

VALERIE: I can get a job and have my own apartment.

CURTIS: On that twenty-five bucks you've got left?

VALERIE: I've got money. I've got another forty I didn't tell you about.

CURTIS: Yeah? Forty that sort of stuck to your fingers while your mom wasn't looking?

VALERIE: Forty I saved! (*She tests other answers.*) I found it. My dad sent it for my birthday.

CURTIS: Okay. Forget it.

VALERIE: If you're in such a hurry to back out, why don't you just get in your daddy's precious pickup and drive off? I don't need this.

CURTIS: Sure you don't. But you needed *me*, Val. You needed the stupid truck to get to Oregon and find your dad, so I took it and got you there. You call that backing out?

VALERIE: Okay! (*She slings an apple core away, just missing him.*) I needed you. I used you. Sue me.

CURTIS: Val—I'm not mad at you! I'm just telling you something. Your dad's not going to take you in. (*He picks up her apple core and puts it in the trash can.*) Listen, you don't have to talk about it till you're ready. But you've got to rethink your plans now. It's not going to be the way you were dreaming it. (*She begins to pace rapidly.*) What are you doing?

VALERIE: Exercising. (*She marches up and down, swinging her arms.* CURTIS *and the* MODOC SENTRIES *watch, bemused.*) I'm stiff. I hurt.

CURTIS: Why don't you walk around the trail loop? It's just about half a mile.

VALERIE: Because I want to walk around right here. Okay?

CURTIS: Sure. Forget it. (*He returns to his booklet, refusing to look at her.*)

An OLD WOMAN in a shawl and long skirt, gray with time, enters right and brings a small jug to the two SENTRIES. They drink sparingly. When she offers the jug again, they shake their heads and go back to their lookout posts. She hobbles off, left, perhaps to others. Neither CURTIS nor VALERIE take notice.

VALERIE (*looking around, still angry but curious*): What's the trail for, anyway? What's up there? It's just flat.

CURTIS: That's what's strange. It looks like a plain old pasture full of sagebrush. From here you can't tell that the lava is all broken up into crevices and ledges and little caves. It's like World War One up there. Full of trenches.

VALERIE: That book's telling about it?

CURTIS: Yeah. They have them up there in a little box by the trail so you can take a self-guided walk.

VALERIE: Trust you to find a book to stick your nose into, even out here in no-man's-land.

CURTIS: There were people here, once. There were some Indians called Modocs, and they had a war here. Well, more like a siege, I guess you'd say, because about sixty men held off the United States Army for months, holed up in those crevices.

VALERIE (*forgetting to pace*): What for?

CURTIS: Because all this around here was their homeland. But the white settlers wanted it, and got the government to send the Modocs to live on a reservation with another tribe they didn't like. So they ran away, and when the Army ordered them back, they refused, and gathered up their people here in the lava beds to hold out.

VALERIE: You mean women and little kids and everybody?

CURTIS: Yeah, the old folks. The horses and dogs. Everything they had.

VALERIE: What did they eat?

CURTIS (*with a shrug*): What they could find, I guess. And there's a lake back over there. They sneaked down to it at first, but toward the last the soldiers cut off their water supply.

VALERIE *starts to drink the last of the pop, but hesitates, and impulsively offers it to* CURTIS. *He shakes his head. She drinks thoughtfully, looking around.*

VALERIE: Why the blazes didn't the Army just let them *have* their stupid hunk of land and save everybody a lot of trouble?

As she speaks, the two SENTRIES *stand up warily as a small tattered group of* MODOC MEN *and* WOMEN *gathers between them. Two tall imposing men are obviously rival leaders, unable to agree about something. They mime an argument. Their supporters, anxiously watching, slowly divide into separate sides.*

CURTIS: Yeah, that's what some people back east wondered. (*He waves the booklet, which has given him the story.*) So finally they sent out five people to be, like, a peace committee or something, to try to talk.

The FIRST LEADER *defends his position passionately, but the* SECOND LEADER *senses weakness in him, and suddenly grabs a woman's shawl and drapes it over his rival's head. The* FIRST LEADER, *shocked, throws it off, but he has been called a coward. His followers back away from him.*

CURTIS: But it turned out the Modocs had broken up into two groups with two chiefs. One chief kept trying to work things out. But the other groups just— stood up at a meeting and blew away a general and a minister from the peace party. Naturally the Army said, "That does it— not a *general*," and started lobbing mortar shells into the hideout every fifteen minutes. Like, this is *war*, man—no more shilly-shally stuff.

In deep anguish the FIRST LEADER *reluctantly agrees with the* SECOND, *who hurries off triumphantly with his men. The little gray crowd melts away. In sharp contrast to* CURTIS'S *flippant comment, the* FIRST LEADER *sinks to his knees in despair.*

VALERIE (*rubbing her shoulders*): It's cold here. The sun's about to go down, isn't it? How do you suppose they stayed warm in this place?

CURTIS: I guess they had woven mats and things. Blankets. Some of the ledges and little cubbyholes maybe kept off part of the rain and snow. But it must have been hard, surrounded in here. And nothing much to make fires with.

VALERIE: You think we could make a fire?

CURTIS (*looking around*)**:** I guess it wouldn't hurt. You're supposed to be in a campsite, and it looks like somebody made a fire once, here in these rocks. See if you can find some dead sagebrush or something. (*They leave in opposite directions.*)

A SHAMAN[3] *appears, wearing a gray tunic, his head bound with a white cloth. The* SENTRIES *give him rapt attention. The broken* LEADER, *still kneeling, bends his forehead to the ground like someone badly beaten who refuses to fall. The* SHAMAN *lifts his*

3. **Shaman** [shä′mən]: a Native American healer who acts as both priest and doctor.

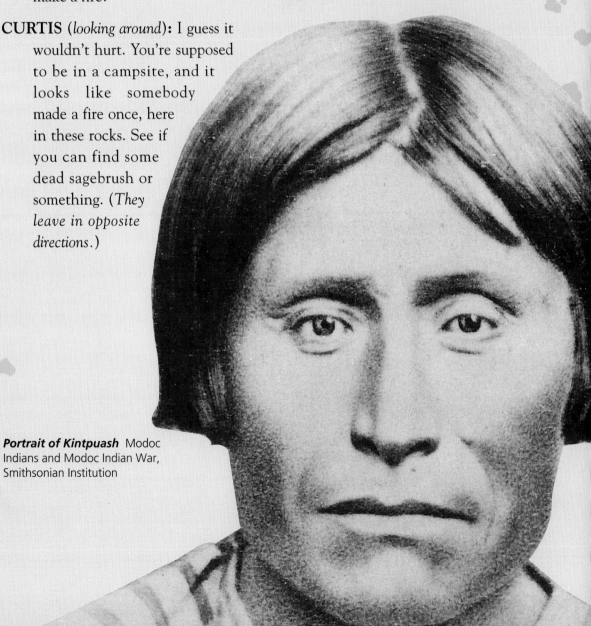

Portrait of Kintpuash Modoc Indians and Modoc Indian War, Smithsonian Institution

arms reverently to the sky. One hand holds a medicine stick about four feet long. Feathers, fur, beads, and charms hang from it on a thong. He plants the stick on a rocky ridge, faces the four points of the compass, and leaves. CURTIS and VALERIE return with some small dry branches.

VALERIE: Like this?

CURTIS: Yeah, this might do it, with a little dry grass twisted up to start with. (*He lays a fire and nods toward the tote hanging from her shoulder.*) You got any matches in that bag-lady collection of junk?

VALERIE: You know I don't smoke. Don't you have some in the truck?

CURTIS: Bound to. (*He goes to look.* VALERIE *turns slowly, her eyes passing over the* MODOC LEADER *and the medicine stick. She rubs her arms, still cold.*)

VALERIE: Curtis? (*She kneels to break up some twigs.*) It's eerie out here.

CURTIS (*returning*): Not one stupid match anywhere. My dad doesn't smoke either, and I guess he just—(*He kicks the pile of twigs.*) We're real pioneers,

man. (*He hands her a sweater he has brought.*) I found this, though.

VALERIE: I don't need it.

CURTIS: Hey, put it on. You're shivering.

VALERIE (*laying her feather on the table and pulling the sweater over her head*): You don't have to be nice to me.

CURTIS (*exasperated*): Was I being nice? Sorry! I keep forgetting myself and doing weird things my parents taught me. It won't happen again, I promise.

VALERIE (*too serious to play along*): You are nice, Curt. Face it.

CURTIS: And that's what gave you the idea in the first place.

VALERIE: What idea?

CURTIS: The big idea to come on to me like I was suddenly a new invention you couldn't live without.

VALERIE: What are you talking about? You have a really twitchy mind, Curtis. Always cranking corners and throwing people off balance.

CURTIS: You know what I'm talking

about. You needed a way to get to Oregon and track down your dad. You didn't have the guts or money to hop a bus and do it yourself. But you didn't mind working *me* over for a couple of weeks till I was ga-ga-gooey enough to steal a truck and head off, any direction you pointed to. You want Oregon? Sure, I'll just go tearing right up the middle of California on this screaming freeway like I know what I'm doing.

VALERIE: You knew what you were doing. Don't try blaming me for that part of it. You wanted to run as bad as I did. You didn't like the way you were living any more than I did.

CURTIS: Nothing was wrong with the way I was living.

VALERIE: That's the whole point, stupid. You've been this nice quiet decent kid with the good grades—forever! You never had a problem because you never make a wave. Curtis—you needed to make a *wave*. A number-nine wave, to see if it was going to drown you or if you could ride it in.

CURTIS: Yeah? (*He sits on the table,* as far as he can get from her.) That's really dumb stuff to think.

VALERIE: No, that dumb stuff is the truth. I did use you, Curt—I admit it. But you used me, too. To test yourself. Am I right? This whole trip has been your test. (*He shrugs and twists the empty paper sack into lumps, unable to meet her eyes. She studies him, her voice going softer.*) Didn't it ever bother you? To *always* do what was expected of you?

CURTIS (*with difficulty*): Sure. I guess it bothered me. I guess I thought about it, when my folks started planning my life for me, or things like that.

VALERIE: But you didn't do anything about it, Curt.

CURTIS (*giving his life a long slow look, and almost smiling at its ironies*): Not till now. Not till Miss Valerie Vroom-Vroom put the whammy on me.

VALERIE: Is that a compliment? (*She sits beside him on the table, moved by his pain.*) You know what made me sad when I first noticed you in school? The way

Portrait of Kaitchkona Modoc Indians and Modoc Indian War, Smithsonian Institution

you always seemed like you needed to put yourself down. Just because you were serious and kind and curious about things, and—sort of, you know, in love with life. *Besides* being smart and nice. I couldn't understand that, how you could be all those special things and still always seem like you didn't like who you were.

CURTIS: What's so smart and nice about this mess?

VALERIE: Oh, great, Curt. (*The* SENTRIES *stop searching the horizon and lean quietly on their long rifles, curious.*) I know you don't think taking your dad's truck was a really smart idea. Or selling your watch yesterday to get the radiator fixed. But I—I realize you're here in a lava bed with me and the Murdocks because you wanted to help me be happier. That's nice.

CURTIS: Modocs. Not Murdock. Mo-doc.

VALERIE (*softly*): Okay. Whatever.

The SENTRIES *smile at each other. The defeated* LEADER *gets to his knees and stares into emptiness, perhaps seeing his people's future.*

CURTIS: I'm sorry the way things turned out for you this morning. Maybe your dad had his reasons for whatever he said, but—man, when you got back to the truck, I thought—the way you looked—I thought he'd socked you in the mouth or something.

VALERIE: You did? No—he didn't lay a finger on me. Not even a handshake. I was a real shock to him, I guess. He opens the door and there I am, like Hi, I'm Valerie and I've come to live with you, Dad. And his eyes go, Valerie Who?

CURTIS: Yeah. I guess without any warning like that, what could you expect? But when you went in, what happened?

VALERIE: Nothing. He asked how was I. He said he was just about to leave for work. That's what really got to me the most. When he looked at his watch.

TWO WOMEN *enter and kneel on either side of the* LEADER. *One hands him a morsel of food. He pushes it away, not angrily but so abruptly that it falls from her hand. The* WOMEN *crouch constrained until he finally sighs deeply and holds out his hands to them so they can help him rise. They guide him slowly out of sight.*

CURTIS: But when you explained to him. How things were, and all—

VALERIE: He said it was a bad idea. He asked if my mom had put me up to it. Then he looked at his watch again. Damn—he could've faked it! He could've pretended he was glad to see me, and really wished I could stay with him, but golly gee, he was just starting a three-year job at the South Pole or something and he'd see me when he got back.

CURTIS: He didn't know how to handle it, Val.

VALERIE: He ought to have tried. It would've helped a lot if I could remember he tried. Even *I* take the trouble to lie if it'll make things—not hurt so much! Couldn't he?

CURTIS: Maybe he thought it would be easier on you if he just said right out you couldn't stay with him.

VALERIE: He didn't even *try*.

CURTIS: You scared him, Val. You made him feel—defensive and stuff.

VALERIE: Why do people get that way? Why can't they sit down and say, "Let's talk. Let's listen. Till we understand each other?" What the blazes is so hard about that?

CURTIS: I don't know, Val.

One of the SENTRIES *ventures out to find the morsel of food, picks the debris off, and shares it with his companion. They eat hungrily and lick their fingers as they return to their posts.*

VALERIE (*staring into the distance*): It feels so strange. All these years my dad's been out there, like some kind of magic spell I could make. I knew no matter how bad things got, all I had to say was "Hey, I don't have to take this. I can go live with him." And now . . . (*She struggles to keep her voice even.*) All at once there's not any magic to call on anymore.

CURTIS (*hurting with her*): Maybe he'll feel different someday. Maybe even the fact that you came to him and asked—

VALERIE: It's going to snow, isn't it? The sky's so heavy. We're going to be found here frozen to a picnic table, all white and ghosty.

CURTIS (*briskly, relieved that she has regained control*): Yeah, it feels really strange to be cold, when you stop to think that all this rock that we're walking around on out here was flowing once, red hot, pouring out over trees and grass, and nothing could stop it. (*As he speaks, he goes off left to the truck and returns with a dark bundle.*) And all these little mountains were cinder cones, and the ashes—

VALERIE (*interrupting*): What's that?

CURTIS: Wrap up in it. You're still shivering.

VALERIE: It's a sleeping bag. (*Shakily, she chooses to laugh instead of cry.*) Oh, man, Curt. Just one sleeping bag? You were thinking ahead, weren't you?

CURTIS (*surprised into defensiveness*): What's that mean? No. Hey, people take sleeping bags. When they go hunting or something. In case they get stranded or something.

VALERIE: In case they get lucky or something. Were you making big plans for us?

CURTIS: I don't know what you mean. Yeah, I do, but—Okay. It occurred to me. Just wrap up in it. Things turned out different. Okay?

VALERIE (*wrapping herself in it gratefully*): Thanks. (*She hunts inside it.*) I've lost one of my earrings.

CURTIS: No. You lost it while you were asleep in the truck. (*He pats his shirt pocket.*) I've got it.

VALERIE (*studying his face*): Oh. (*She wraps herself tightly again.*) I keep thinking about the children, and the old ones. How hard they had it. When it wasn't their fault. Have you read far enough to know what happened?

CURTIS (*referring to the booklet*): Well, the siege lasted like three or four months, with these sixty guys holding off twelve hundred soldiers. But they were nearly starving, and when they tried to escape to the south over there, they got captured in little groups.

VALERIE: Didn't they ever get their homeland?

CURTIS (*shaking his head*): The settlers got it.

VALERIE: But it's empty. Couldn't they have *shared* it, even?

CURTIS (*rolling the booklet into a tight cylinder*): I guess not. And the Army figured hanging the leaders would set the right example. So they did.

VALERIE: Oh, man, that's sad. That's so stupid and sad.

CURTIS: It said when the Army came in here, afterward, they found like this stick that the medicine man had propped up in the rocks. It was supposed to give the Indians victory, you know—stop the bullets and all that. Only it hadn't.

VALERIE: Whatever happened to the other Murdocks?

CURTIS: The Mo—I don't know. It didn't say.

VALERIE (*suddenly bending forward in pain*): Why couldn't he want me, Curt? Why couldn't he be glad I was his kid and wanted to live with him? It stinks. (*She begins to cry.*) It really stinks.

CURTIS: Hey, Val. Don't do that. Listen. Hold out. (*He can't even take her hidden hand.*) You've got to just—hold out. Till it gets better.

VALERIE (*bitterly, still crying*): You figure four months of holding out would do it, Curt? Like the Murdocks?

CURTIS: They tried, Val. Aren't you glad they tried?

VALERIE: But it wasn't enough.

CURTIS: You tried, too, Val. This morning—

VALERIE: But it didn't help.

CURTIS: Listen to me. I was proud of you this morning, walking up to your dad's door. You're brave—don't ever forget how brave. And you're way ahead of

the Modocs—they had their troubles a hundred years ago, but you're right here—alive, with everything still ahead for you. (*She grows quiet as he stumbles on, distressed.*) There's got to be better things out there, and love, and—I wish I was the one, because the way I feel about you—I mean these really deep feelings—but right now what they're like is—friendship. I don't know if that means anything to you, but if it does . . .

VALERIE (*calmly*): You want me to give up.

CURTIS: No. Just go back. And hold out. That's all.

VALERIE (*testing reality*): Are your folks going to give you hell?

CURTIS: I don't know. Usually they act like "Okay, we see your point." So this is scary, because I don't know if they'll be that way. Because this time we're talking really major—(*He turns to her with a small proud smile.*) A really major wave. (*She smiles back faintly, giving him the courage to go on.*) You got to remember it's not all your mom's fault either, Val. She's got a right to her own kind of life. I know you think your dad's a real free spirit and all that, but he shouldn't have bailed out on her—he owed you something—

VALERIE (*holding the truth away*): You know what's funny? All this time I wasn't even thinking about the soldiers. You know? All the soldiers that probably got killed here. Boys from New Jersey or someplace, lying out there on lava rock with bullet holes in them, wondering how their lives turned out so crazy.

CURTIS: Val, if there's maybe times when you need to talk to somebody older than just me, my folks are mostly pretty reasonable. Pretty understanding. Okay?

VALERIE (*trusting him*): Yeah, Curt. I can tell they must be. It rubbed off on you. (*She stands up and lets the sleeping bag fall.*) I think I want to walk the trail.

CURTIS: You do? Okay. Yeah.

VALERIE: Before it gets too dark.

CURTIS: Okay. Sure. (*He bundles up the sleeping bag in such a burst of gratitude that he breaks one of the ties that holds the bag in a roll.*)

VALERIE (*hesitating*): Then, maybe . . . There's not much point in sitting in the cab of a truck all night in the snow.

CURTIS (*gladly giving her time*): Well, probably not.

VALERIE (*with difficulty*): So. We can head back down toward L.A., I guess. It's not like I'm giving up. Or—or settling for just anything. It's just how things are for now. Okay? (*She walks off toward the trail.*)

CURTIS (*almost reaching toward her*): Okay. It's kind of rough there at first. Go slow. (*She disappears. He stares after her through several moments of silence.*) Val? You okay?

VALERIE (*from offstage*): Yeah.

CURTIS (*calling, now*): Don't trip on the rocks—they're sharp. Just take it slow. (*He catches a glimpse of her.*) Hey, you look like a ghost floating along up there.

VALERIE (*from farther away*): I do? I'm going on around the loop now, Curt. I'll see you.

CURTIS (*calling*): Yeah. I'll be here.

He waits, but there is silence. In it, the drum begins to beat again, a deep heartthrob. He turns his head almost as though he hears it and is seeking its source. He draws a deep breath. With the sleeping bag's broken cord he ties together Valerie's feather, the pop can, and his booklet, and attaches the cord to the stick he used on his hike. He props the stick up on the table with a pile of rocks, and slowly hangs Valerie's earring with the other charms. As he works, MODOCS appear, beginning a slow exodus, burdened with bundles. They pass behind him, gray and spent, the young ones helping the old, the spared ones carrying the wounded.

CURTIS (*softly, in an ordinary voice*): Just hold out, Val. Okay? Because you can make it. You can. You're going to. I love you, Valerie. But that's for later, when there's not so much to fight.

He gathers up the paper sacks and sleeping bag to stow in the truck, and waits, facing the spot where she will reappear. A dwindling line of INDIANS continues to pass in the growing darkness. The two SENTRIES are the last to go. As the drum stops, they glance back at the two medicine sticks standing bravely in the only light that is left.

CURTAIN

OUIDA SEBESTYEN

Ouida Sebestyen was born in 1924 in Vernon, Texas, where she grew up. She says about her home town, "When my life got too small . . . I enlarged it at the library or the movies. My favorite dream was to sit in a theater someday, watching people react with gasps and laugher to a story I had created."

Sebestyen made a long leap for college and attended the University of Colorado. She wrote her first novel when she was twenty— but it was thirty-five years before any of her work was published. "After four unaccepted novels and four hundred rejection slips for stories, plays, poems—even true confessions—I finally got the hang of it."

When Sebestyen writes, she listens "to ragtime or whatever music my characters might listen to." She writes in longhand first. "Then I type, revising like mad, over and over."

FROM NARRATIVE OF THE LIFE OF
FREDERICK DOUGLASS
AN AMERICAN SLAVE

FREDERICK DOUGLASS

Frederick Douglass Series No. 22 Jacob Lawrence, gouache on paper, Hampton University Museum, Hampton, Virginia

My master's family consisted of two sons, Andrew and Richard; one daughter, Lucretia, and her husband, Captain Thomas Auld. They lived in one house, upon the home plantation of Colonel Edward Lloyd. My master was Colonel Lloyd's clerk and superintendent. He was what might be called the overseer of the overseers. I spent two years of childhood on this plantation in my old master's family. It was here that I witnessed the bloody transaction recorded in the first chapter; and as I received my first impressions of slavery on this plantation, I will give some description of it, and of slavery as it there existed. The plantation is about twelve miles north of Easton, in Talbot county, and is situated on the border of Miles River. The principal products raised upon it were tobacco, corn, and wheat. These were raised in great abundance; so that, with the products of this and the other farms belonging to him, he was able to keep in almost constant employment a large sloop,[1] in carrying them to market at Baltimore. This sloop was named Sally Lloyd, in honor of one of the colonel's daughters. My master's son-in-law, Captain Auld, was master of the vessel; she was otherwise manned by the colonel's own slaves. Their names were Peter, Isaac, Rich, and Jake. These were esteemed very highly by the other slaves, and looked upon as the privileged ones of the plantation; for it was no small affair, in the eyes of the slaves, to be allowed to see Baltimore.

Colonel Lloyd kept from three to four hundred slaves on his home plantation, and owned a large number more on the neighboring farms belonging to him. The names of the farms nearest to the home plantation were Wye Town and New Design. "Wye Town" was under the

1. **sloop** [slüp]: a sailboat with one mast and several sails.

overseership of a man named Noah Willis. New Design was under the overseership of a Mr. Townsend. The overseers of these, and all the rest of the farms, numbering over twenty, received advice and direction from the managers of the home plantation. This was the great business place. It was the seat of government for the whole twenty farms. All disputes among the overseers were settled here. If a slave was convicted of any high misdemeanor,[2] became unmanageable, or evinced[3] a determination to run away, he was brought immediately here, severely whipped, put on board the sloop, carried to Baltimore, and sold to Austin Woolfolk, or some other slave-trader, as a warning to the slaves remaining.

Here, too, the slaves of all the other farms received their monthly allowance of food, and their yearly clothing. The men and women slaves received, as their monthly allowance of food, eight pounds of pork, or its equivalent in fish, and one bushel of corn meal. Their yearly clothing consisted of two coarse linen shirts, one pair of linen trousers, like the shirts, one jacket, one pair of trousers for winter, made of coarse negro cloth, one pair of stockings, and one pair of shoes; the whole of which could not have cost more than seven dollars. The allowance of the slave children was given to their mothers, or the old women having the care of them. The children unable to work in the field had neither shoes, stockings, jackets, nor trousers, given to them; their clothing consisted of two coarse linen shirts per year. When these failed them, they went naked until the next allowance-day. Children from seven to ten years old, of both sexes, almost naked, might be seen at all seasons of the year.

There were no beds given the slaves, unless one coarse blanket be considered such, and none but the men and women had these. This, however, is not considered a very great privation. They find less difficulty from the want of beds, than from the want of time to sleep; for when their day's work in the field is done, the most of them having their washing, mending, and cooking to do, and having few or none

2. **misdemeanor** [mis′ di mē′ nər]: misbehavior.
3. **evinced** [i vinsd′]: showed clearly.

of the ordinary facilities for doing either of these, very many of their sleeping hours are consumed in preparing for the field the coming day; and when this is done, old and young, male and female, married and single, drop down side by side, on one common bed,—the cold, damp floor,—each covering himself or herself with their miserable blankets; and here they sleep till they are summoned to the field by the driver's horn. At the sound of this, all must rise, and be off to the field. There must be no halting; every one must be at his or her post; and woe betides them who hear not this morning summons to the field; for if they are not awakened by the sense of hearing, they are by the sense of feeling; no age nor sex finds any favor. Mr. Severe, the overseer, used to stand by the door of the quarter, armed with a large hickory stick and heavy cowskin, ready to whip any one who was so unfortunate as not to hear, or, from any other cause, was prevented from being ready to start for the field at the sound of the horn.

Mr. Severe was rightly named: he was a cruel man. I have seen him whip a woman, causing the blood to run half an hour at the time; and this, too, in the midst of her crying children, pleading for their mother's release. He seemed to take pleasure in manifesting his fiendish barbarity. Added to his cruelty, he was a profane swearer. It was enough to chill the blood and stiffen the hair of an ordinary man to hear him talk. Scarce a sentence escaped him but that was commenced or concluded by some horrid oath. The field was the place to witness his cruelty and profanity. His presence made it both the field of blood and of blasphemy. From the rising till the going down of the sun, he was cursing, raving, cutting, and slashing among the slaves of the field, in the most frightful manner. His career was short. He died very soon after I went to Colonel Lloyd's; and he died as he lived, uttering, with his dying groans, bitter curses and horrid oaths. His death was regarded by the slaves as the result of a merciful providence.

Mr. Severe's place was filled by a Mr. Hopkins. He was a very different man. He was less cruel, less profane, and made less noise, than Mr. Severe. His course was characterized by no extraordinary demonstrations of cruelty. He whipped, but seemed to take no pleasure in it. He was called by the slaves a good overseer.

**Frederick Douglass Series
No. 22** Jacob Lawrence,
Hampton University Museum,
Hampton, Virginia

The home plantation of Colonel Lloyd wore the appearance of a
country village. All the mechanical operations for all the farms were
performed here. The shoemaking and mending, the blacksmithing,
cartwrighting,[4] coopering,[5] weaving, and grain-grinding, were all
performed by the slaves on the home plantation. The whole place

4. **cartwrighting** [kärt′ rīt ing]: making carts.
5. **coopering** [kü′ pər ing]: making or repairing barrels.

wore a business-like aspect very unlike the neighboring farms. The number of houses, too, conspired to give it advantage over the neighboring farms. It was called by the slaves the *Great House Farm*. Few privileges were esteemed higher, by the slaves of the out-farms, than that of being selected to do errands at the Great House Farm. It was associated in their minds with greatness. A representative could not be prouder of his election to a seat in the American Congress, than a slave on one of the out-farms would be of his election to do errands at the Great House Farm. They regarded it as evidence of great confidence reposed in them by their overseers; and it was on this account, as well as a constant desire to be out of the field from under the driver's lash, that they esteemed it a high privilege, one worth careful living for. He was called the smartest and most trusty fellow, who had this honor conferred upon him the most frequently. The competitors for this office sought as diligently to please their overseers, as the office-seekers in the political parties seek to please and deceive the people. The same traits of character might be seen in Colonel Lloyd's slaves, as are seen in the slaves of the political parties.

The slaves selected to go to the Great House Farm, for the monthly allowance for themselves and their fellow-slaves, were peculiarly enthusiastic. While on their way, they would make the dense old woods, for miles around, reverberate with their wild songs, revealing at once the highest joy and the deepest sadness. They would compose and sing as they went along, consulting neither time nor tune. The thought that came up, came out—if not in the word, in the sound;—and as frequently in the one as in the other. They would sometimes sing the most pathetic sentiment in the most rapturous tone, and the most rapturous sentiment in the most pathetic tone. Into all of their songs they would manage to weave something of the Great House Farm. Especially would they do this, when leaving home. They would then sing most exultingly the following words:—

"I am going away to the Great House Farm!
O, yea! O, yea! O!"

from *Narrative of the Life of Frederick Douglass* **87**

This they would sing, as a chorus, to words which to many would seem unmeaning jargon, but which, nevertheless, were full of meaning to themselves. I have sometimes thought that the mere hearing of those songs would do more to impress some minds with the horrible character of slavery, than the reading of whole volumes of philosophy on the subject could do.

I did not, when a slave, understand the deep meaning of those rude and apparently incoherent songs. I was myself within the circle; so that I neither saw nor heard as those without might see and hear. They told a tale of woe which was then altogether beyond my feeble comprehension; they were tones loud, long, and deep; they breathed the prayer and complaint of souls boiling over with the bitterest anguish. Every tone was a testimony against slavery, and a prayer to God for deliverance from chains. The hearing of those wild notes always depressed my spirit, and filled me with ineffable sadness. I have frequently found myself in tears while hearing them. The mere recurrence to those songs, even now, afflicts me; and while I am writing these lines, an expression of feeling has already found its way down my cheek. To those songs I trace my first glimmering conception of the dehumanizing character of slavery. I can never get rid of that conception. Those songs still follow me, to deepen my hatred of slavery, and quicken my sympathies for my brethren in bonds. If any one wishes to be impressed with the soul-killing effects of slavery, let him go to Colonel Lloyd's plantation, and, on allowance-day, place himself in the deep pine woods, and there let him, in silence, analyze the sounds that shall pass through the chambers of his soul,—and if he is not thus impressed, it will only be because "there is no flesh in his obdurate heart."

I have often been utterly astonished, since I came to the north, to find persons who could speak of the singing, among slaves, as evidence of their contentment and happiness. It is impossible to conceive of a greater mistake. Slaves sing most when they are most unhappy. The songs of the slave represent the sorrows of his heart; and he is relieved by them, only as an aching heart is relieved by its tears. At least, such is my experience. I have often sung to drown my sorrow, but seldom to express my happiness. Crying for joy, and singing for joy, were alike uncommon to me while in the jaws of slavery. The singing of a man cast away upon a desolate island might be as appropriately considered as evidence of contentment and happiness, as the singing of a slave; the songs of the one and of the other are prompted by the same emotion.

FREDERICK DOUGLASS

Frederick Douglass [1817-1895] was born into slavery in Tuckahoe, Maryland. Growing up, he learned that the road to freedom and power was through education. Slaves were not taught to read. "Conscious of the difficulty of learning without a teacher, I set out with high hope, and a fixed purpose, at whatever cost or trouble, to learn how to read." After years of copying his young master's copy book, he also learned to write.

When Douglass was about eighteen years old, his first attempt to escape to freedom failed. Three years later, he succeeded in escaping and made his way to New York. There he took the name Frederick Douglass and became known as a famous orator who argued for an end to slavery.

In 1845 he wrote his first autobiography, *Narrative of the Life of Frederick Douglass, an American Slave;* he was to write two more. Two years later, he founded a newspaper, the *North Star*, to carry on the fight against slavery. His beliefs in human rights led him to attend the first women's rights convention.

During the 1860s, he helped recruit for the 54th and 55th Massachusetts Regiment and demanded the right to enlist African American men in the United States Army.

After the Civil War, Douglass served as United States Marshall of the District of Columbia and in 1889 was appointed minister to Haiti. He died in 1895, leaving behind a great legacy of writing and action.

NOVEMBER SERENADE

W. J. Holmes

ike the neighborhood and house, the man was old. The neighborhood had disintegrated past saving. But like the man, the house kept a stiff-backed hint of other, better times.

This morning he woke reluctantly to another dark November day. Then, remembering, he smiled inside. It was the weekend every month Brian came to stay overnight. He liked most of his grandchildren well enough. But Brian, youngest son of his oldest daughter, was special.

The man did the exercises the Veterans Administration Hospital had given him after triple-bypass heart surgery. He shaved, feeling rather than seeing the curve of his lathered jaw in the bathroom mirror. For more than two years he'd been what the VA eye doctor called "functionally unsighted." Meaning legally blind. Meaning glaucoma[1] had nibbled away all but blurred fragments of his vision.

It was still hard to accept, not being able to read half the night or watch World War II movies on late TV. But he still had two good ears for listening to records from the Thirties all the way up into the Sixties. Especially the Big Bands—Artie Shaw, Harry James, Tommy Dorsey, Benny Goodman, Glenn Miller, the Duke, the Count, the others. Plus having little Brian's visits to look forward to. Overall, he got along fine on his own.

1. **glaucoma** [glô kō′ mə]: a disease of the eye in which internal pressure results in gradual loss of sight.

He dressed, careful to remember to wear that ugly expensive tweed jacket Brian's mother, Elizabeth Ann, and her fat lawyer husband had given him last Christmas.

Not holding the rail, he walked stiffly down the seventeen steps to the main floor. In the kitchen, his bruised left hand, searching where the stick matches should have been, hit the microwave oven. Ordinarily the useless appliance was hidden on a back shelf in the pantry. But with Elizabeth Ann coming by today he'd brought it out, put it on the counter, forgotten it.

He glared at the gray blur that was the microwave. The family had meant well, saying how it could save him time, which he already had plenty of. The thing was, the whole idea of cooking food in seconds without fire made him queasy to his stomach.

The phone rang. It was that woman from Elder-Aid volunteers.

"Hi, Billy. Just checking to see if my favorite senior citizen needed anything."

She meant well. They all did. But he didn't want their help. Why couldn't people understand pride?

"I'm all right. Don't need anything. Goodbye."

He finally found the matchbox on the gritty linoleum floor, and lit the back burners of the gas stove.

Whistling "Deep Purple" (why didn't people whistle anymore?), he made breakfast. Real coffee, strong, with three spoons of sugar. Two fried eggs. Buttered toast and jam. The VA dietitian had warned him what that kind of food did to his cholesterol. Or maybe it was triglycerides.[2] But his father had eaten eggs for breakfast all his adult

2. **triglycerides** [trī glis′ ə rīdz]: fatty acids, blood fats.

life and died in his own bed upstairs, age ninety-one. Dietitians, like doctors, were fine when they stuck to curing sick people. But until he got sick again, he knew what was best for him. Why couldn't people understand that?

The old man turned off the stove, turned on the radio to the FM station that was mostly ads, weather, and time, plus what the pimply voiced announcers called Golden Oldies music. The forecast was strong winds with rain or snow flurries. Time, 9:43. And today's Golden Oldies started with Charlie Spivak's band, which the announcer bet very few listeners would remember. The old man remembered. He'd gone with his late wife to hear Charlie Spivak at the Civic Arena in 1944, just before being drafted and shipped out for Europe. Just in time for the Bulge[3] in Belgium in December of 1944. Now there was being cold!

The phone rang. A loud baritone said, "Good morning. We're calling a selectfew homeowners in your section of the city. About siding."

Ordinarily, he let phone salespeople finish their pitch, both because it made a break in the long day's silence and because phone selling had to be a lousy way to make a living. But this day with Brian to get ready for he was short: "Not in the market."

"How can you know that without—"

Shaking his bald head, the old man hung up, waited. It rang

3. **Bulge, Battle of the**: final major German counteroffensive in World War II.

Stardreams

Theme of
CHARLIE SPIVAK
AND HIS ORCHESTRA
The man who plays the sweetest trumpet in the world.

MUSIC BY
DEE
SPIVAK
URKE

Sincerely,
Charlie Spivak

MUTUAL MUSIC SOCIETY, Inc.
1270 SIXTH AVENUE, NEW YORK, N.Y.

again—the loud salesman. The old man said, "Telephone harassment is a crime. I'll bring in the phone company or the police if you bother me again. Go get a real job."

He hung up, the phone rang, but this time it was Elizabeth Ann. After all the years, she sounded so much like her mother that his useless eyes misted.

"Dad. Quick call to see if you needed anything when I come by this afternoon. How are you?"

"Fine. How's Brian?"

"Allergies. Otherwise okay. And about Brian."

"What about Brian? Is he sick again?"

"Oh, no. We can talk when I see you this afternoon. And Dad."

"What?"

"Remember me telling you about Haven Rest Apartments? They have an opening. Dad, it's not just another—"

"Old-folks' home. Yes it is."

"But won't you even look at it? Every Haven Rest tenant has a living room, kitchen, bath and shower, bedroom. Security system. R.N. on call . . . ."

"You're reading from a brochure. No."

The dreaded angry silence lengthened between him and the person in all the world, next to Brian, he cared most about. At last, she said, "Dad."

"Yes."

"If it's money."

"It isn't," although it was that, too.

"All the family agrees. Living alone in that big old barn of a house. In a neighborhood I don't even like to drive through in daylight. All those new people moving in on what used to be such a beautiful part of the city."

"When your grandparents moved into this neighborhood, they were New People. From the Old Country. Give them a chance."

"Dad."

"Yes."

"The family worries. We just want what's best for you."

"Then leave me alone in my home."

Elizabeth Ann, crying, hung up. He went into the parlor, putting on a stack of scratchy records, saving for last that favorite Benny Goodman album.

He stood there listening, smiling, as "Don't Be That Way" and then "Rose Room" spoke of happier times, of dancing with his late wife. Turning up the volume very loud, he Hoovered the whole downstairs without resting. Then dishes, piled up for days.

He smashed a cup. Sweeping up the pieces by feel, hiding the broken parts under the leaky sink, he thought: A man shouldn't have to sneak around this way in his own home.

He was breathing fast and shallow. Sweating. But no warning pressure on his ribbed chest, reminding him of the frail cardiovascular system inside there. But just in case, he slipped one of the tiny nitro[4] pills under his tongue.

The radio reported it was 1 P.M., eighty percent chance of rain or snow, wind twenty-five miles an hour out of the northwest. And he still had the errand to run.

The thing was, last Tuesday he'd forgotten to put on his list for the Elder-Aid shopper to buy treats for little Brian for that night. Without self-pity he thought: I wonder how much talking with Grandpa and how much the junk food counts in Brian's visits? About equal parts, he guessed.

The nearest thing to a grocery left in the decaying neighborhood was that convenience store-gas station, eight blocks away. He got a shaky feeling just thinking about eight blocks of broken, slippery sidewalk, passing strangers he couldn't see anymore except as skewed gray blurs.

But he couldn't disappoint Brian.

And there was time enough to stretch out on the saggy sofa, let muscles and mind relax, listen to records. With a need for other voices than his own, he reached behind the neatly stacked Big Bands collections for some Sinatra, Ella Fitzgerald, Sarah Vaughan, Nat Cole, Satchmo.

---

4. **nitro** [nī′ trō]: (nitroglycerine) medicine that dilates blood vessels.

The rest, the voices that did things to lyrics like nobody before or since, were healing. Feeling tired but all right he dressed against the weather. Checked left pants pocket for the hoarded $20 bill. Ready as he'd ever be.

The careful curb-feeling walk wasn't all that bad for five of the eight blocks. Then he sucked icy air, got a fit of coughing, strength emptying out of him like water out of a combat boot. He found a slow, wheezing military rhythm. Hut-two-three-four. Hut-two-three-four. Finally there was only a single block left and everything was going to be all right.

Near where the convenience store door had to be, the old man's boots began crunching mounds of broken glass.

"Hi, Billy."

The voice was the police officer's who'd patrolled the dying neighborhood for it must be twenty years. He said it was the third time the new people running the store had been hit. Both beat up bad. "Either neighborhood kids are getting meaner, or it's different punks."

"How do you know it was kids?" the old man asked.

The police officer didn't answer that. Instead he said, "Sorry, Billy, can't let you in the store until the Juvenile team comes to check it out. Jump in the squad car where it's warm and I'll run you home in a few minutes."

"I can walk."

Turning on careful, rubbery legs, the old man began feeling his way home. Only now the cutting wind was in his face and it was worse than in the Bulge in Belgium in 1944.

He fell, got up.

He lost track of time and space for a while. Then he blundered into a wall, high and stucco-rough, that was the corner of his street and Fremont Avenue. Only three more blocks, he thought, marching very slowly now but moving, hut-two-three-four, sound off, so cold, so scared.

The mugger took him down from behind, face in the frozen ground, easily holding both the old man's arms behind his back, not hurting more than necessary to rummage through pockets, finding the hoarded $20 that was to be for Brian's bedtime treat.

Then the mugger was gone. The old man lay face down for a while, breathing icy air, hoping a rare passing car would stop instead of speeding away, not to get involved.

Finally he made it shakily to his feet. Oriented to direction home by the awful wind in his face. Two blocks. One, the warning pressure on his chest bad. The long, once-elegant driveway, snow drifting thinly.

Home.

Inside, he sat carefully on the saving warmth of the kitchen radiator. Exhaustion, in waves, kept flooding through his wheezing chest.

Go rest. Only, first, this to do. Important!

He fumbled for the telephone. Slowly, with infinite care, he peeled the glove off his left hand. Flexed fingers. Dialed.

"Elizabeth Ann, it's Dad."

"Are you all right? Your voice sounds funny."

"Caught a little cold. That or flu. Elizabeth Ann, would Brian be too disappointed not to come stay the weekend with me?"

"I'm sure he wouldn't." The relief in her voice was open. She was like her mother, couldn't hide her feelings. "I mean, he'll be disappointed, of course. But he'll understand. Dad are you sure you're okay? You sound funny."

"So do you. Must be the connection. Elizabeth Ann?"

"Yes?"

"I've been thinking. About Brian coming every month. Oh, he's special to me, you know that."

"I know."

"But getting ready every month. . . ."

"I know. And maybe he and I could stop by for shorter visits, more often."

"That'd be fine. Well, I've got to go."

"Goodbye, Dad. I love you."

"I know. Goodbye."

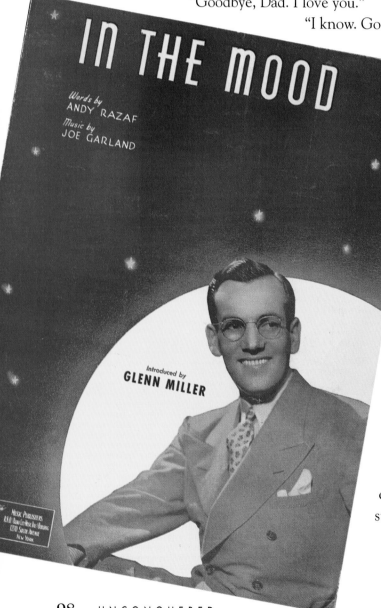

He fumbled the receiver back on its cradle. Sat for a long time more on the radiator. Reached to where he kept the extra supply of heart pills. He got to his feet. Waited for the dizzy spell to pass. The thudding chest was calmer. The silence—the thought of the long weekend of silence without Brian—was bad.

In the parlor he put on Glenn Miller. "In the Mood." "String of Pearls." "Moonlight Serenade." He knew all the lyrics, not forgetting a single word after all the years.

The early November evening came. Outside it was still snowing. But in his house it was warm, as secure as life was going to get anymore. For supper he had a peanut butter sandwich, strong black coffee.

"It's not going to be so bad," he said out loud, putting the albums in place to be able to find them again.

Not holding to the railing, he climbed the seventeen steps to the second floor and went to bed with his radio tuned to the Golden Oldies station. Just before he slept, the radio played one of Benny Goodman's early hits.

Martha Tilton—he remembered the vocalist's name after fifty years. Liltin' Martha Tilton, they'd called her. And still hurting, but nothing he couldn't handle, the old man went to sleep. In his own bed. In his own home.

W . J .   H O L M E S

Wilfred Jay Holmes was born in 1900 in Stockport, New York, and graduated from the United States Naval Academy. His navy career lasted from 1918 to 1946, when he retired as a captain. While in the navy, he taught engineering and mathematics at the University of Hawaii and continued to teach there for many years after his retirement.

While in the service, Holmes wrote under the name of Alec Hudson. Most of his work deals with naval warfare. His best-known books are *Battle Stations, Enemy Sighted, Rendezvous, and Undersea Victory.*

MY PEOPLE ARE A MULTITUDE OF ONE

NANCY WOOD

My people are a multitude of one.
Many voices are within them.
Many lives they have lived as various Beings.
They could have been a bear, a lion, an eagle or even
A rock, a river or a tree.   5
Who knows?
All of these Beings are within them.
They can use them any time they want.
On some days it is good to be a tree
Looking out in all directions at once.   10
On some days it is better to be a rock
Saying nothing and blind to everything.
On some days the only thing to do is
To fight fiercely like a lion.
Then, too, there are reasons for being an eagle.   15
When life becomes too hard here
My people can fly away and see
How small the earth really is.
Then they can laugh and come back home again.

Conventionalized Bird with Rain Clouds Oqwa Pi, watercolor, 12" x 18",
San Ildefonso Pueblo, New Mexico

N A N C Y   W O O D

Nancy Wood was born in Trenton, New Jersey, in 1936. She studied first at Bucknell University, and then at the University of Colorado. Her first book, *Central City*, was followed by other books about the West—novels, nonfiction, and poetry. Among them: *Little Wrangler, Colorado, Hollering Sun*, and *Clearcut: The Deforestation of America*. Many of her books are illustrated with photographs by her former husband, Myron Wood. Nancy Wood makes her home in Colorado.

Asking Big Questions About the Literature

LITERATURE STUDY

Point of View

Authors choose a **point of view,** or vantage point, from which to present the action in their stories.

A *first-person narrator* is a character in the story who tells the story as he or she experiences it and uses pronouns such as *I, me, we, us,* and *ours.* A *third-person limited narrator* is a character who tells the story through his or her eyes and uses pronouns such as *he, she, they, them,* and *theirs.* A *third-person omniscient* (all-knowing) narrator also tells the story in the third person.

In this unit, the point of view enhances your understanding of survival. Make a chart to identify the main character and the point of view of each nonfiction selection and short story you've read in this unit. (*See "Point of View" on page 118.*)

Ask THE CHARACTERS

Each character in this unit is a survivor—someone who has held onto life *despite* challenges and obstacles. Choose several characters whose survival stories you admire. For each character, write a definition of survival from that character's point of view. Now write a one-sentence definition of survival that combines these various points of view.

Say It in Pictures

A famous expression says, "A picture is worth a thousand words." One illustration, that is, communicates more meaning than many words. Choose two selections from this unit in which the art that accompanies the selection plays a major role in your understanding of the story. For each selection, write a paragraph that explains *how* and *why* the art helps you understand the meaning of survival in the selection.

Literature	Character	Point of View
I Promised I Would Tell	Sonia Schreiber Weitz	First-Person Narrator

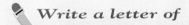
Write a letter of

ADVICE

Based on a selection in this unit, take the role of one character who is a survivor—someone who never gives up. Write a letter of advice to another character in the same selection or in another selection. Describe the qualities, feelings, thoughts, and other supports (such as reliance on friends, family, or faith) that helped you survive. Here is the beginning of a letter that the elderly man in "November Serenade" might have written to Hue Hue in *The Girl in the White Ship*.

Dear Hue Hue,

I know how difficult it is for you to lose your home. I, too, am faced with the loss of my home. But don't give up. Treasure your memories of home so that, when you are far from home, you can keep home with you. . . .

Setting

The **setting** of a story, poem, or play is the time and place in which the action occurs. In this unit, many of the selections are set in a time or place that threatens the survival of a character. Write a descriptive paragraph of a setting from this unit. Use *specific details*, such as dates (1940s) and place-names (Poland), to identify the setting. Use *sensory details*, such has *gloomy, gray,* and *harsh,* to bring the setting to life. (*See "Setting" on page 119.*)

Write a

POEM

The poem "Unconquered and Unconquerable" has a pattern of *rhyme* (making the endings of two or more lines sound alike) and *repetition* (repeating a line in the same form) that makes the poem pleasing to the ear. Using the poem as a model, write another poem about the triumphant spirit of a survivor.

Asking Big Questions About the Literature

What kinds of survival challenges have different cultures faced?

LITERATURE STUDY

Point of View

The poems in this unit are all told from the first-person **point of view**, that is, by a narrator who uses the pronouns *I* or *we*. Make a chart like the one on this page and complete the second column with a phrase identifying the narrator. Then choose a poem, and taking the part of the narrator, prepare an oral presentation in which you describe the survival challenge that you face. (*See* "Point of View" on page 118.)

Write a

POEM

In the early 1500s, Hernán Cortés, a Spanish conquistador, or fortune hunter, conquered the Aztecs, a group of Native Americans living in the Valley of Mexico. In a poem, an anonymous Aztec writer expresses the grief that his people feel for the ruin of their once-beautiful capital, Tenochtitlán. The poem has five stanzas, but the first stanza summarizes the whole story of the poem. Read this stanza. Then, using the words of the Aztec poet as a model, write a *Voices from the Past* poem about one of the groups in this unit.

Broken spears lie in the roads;
we have torn our hair in our grief,
The houses are roofless now, and their walls
are red with blood.

Poem	Voice
"Mother to Son"	Mother speaking to her son
"Unconquered" "We Shall Wait Forever" "My People Are a Multitude of One"	

Why do people threaten one another's survival?

MAKE
A FACT FILE

Choose three or more selections from this unit and identify each of the following people or groups:

- the oppressed (the group or person whose survival is threatened)
- the oppressor (the group or person posing the threat)

Using social-studies textbooks, encyclopedias, and other reference sources, work with a partner or group to make a fact file like the one that has been started for you. Use your fact file to write several paragraphs in which you answer the question, Why does one group threaten the survival of another?

> **Literature Title** "The Girl in the White Ship"
>
> **Oppressed** Hue Hue and her family
>
> **Oppressor** Government of Vietnam
>
> **Fact** In 1975, the Communists of North Vietnam took power in the south. The new government deprived citizens of human rights and freedom.

Write an
EDITORIAL

An **editorial** is a short persuasive essay in which a writer expresses his or her opinion of a news story or event. Write an editorial about a group or person in this unit that threatens another's survival. Use the editorial to convince readers that people should "live and let live."

NOW Choose a Project!

Three projects involving survival are described on the following pages.

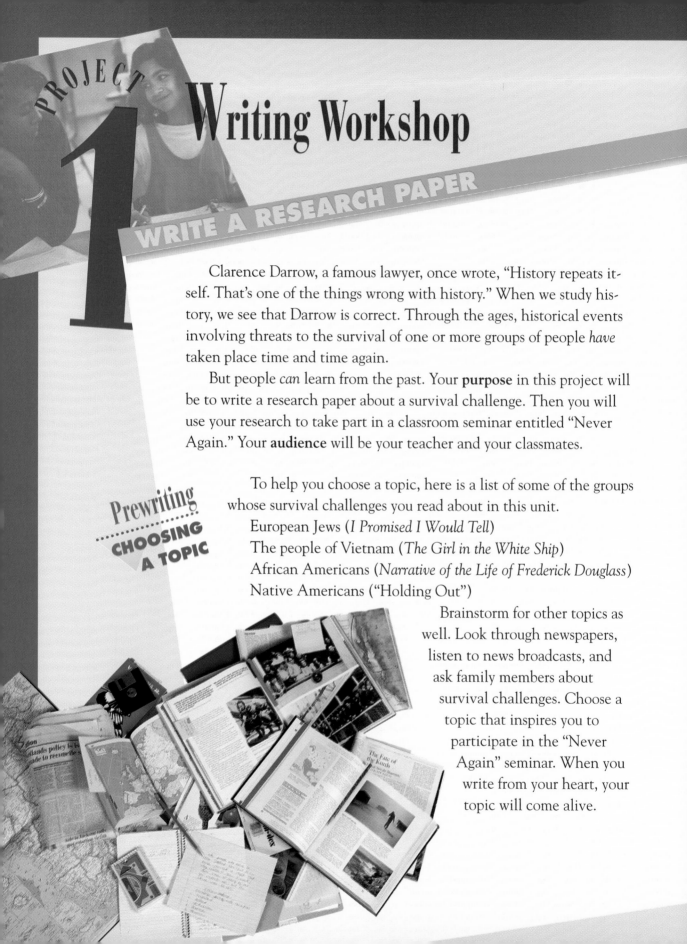

Writing Workshop

WRITE A RESEARCH PAPER

Clarence Darrow, a famous lawyer, once wrote, "History repeats itself. That's one of the things wrong with history." When we study history, we see that Darrow is correct. Through the ages, historical events involving threats to the survival of one or more groups of people *have* taken place time and time again.

But people *can* learn from the past. Your **purpose** in this project will be to write a research paper about a survival challenge. Then you will use your research to take part in a classroom seminar entitled "Never Again." Your **audience** will be your teacher and your classmates.

Prewriting
CHOOSING A TOPIC

To help you choose a topic, here is a list of some of the groups whose survival challenges you read about in this unit.

European Jews (*I Promised I Would Tell*)
The people of Vietnam (*The Girl in the White Ship*)
African Americans (*Narrative of the Life of Frederick Douglass*)
Native Americans ("Holding Out")

Brainstorm for other topics as well. Look through newspapers, listen to news broadcasts, and ask family members about survival challenges. Choose a topic that inspires you to participate in the "Never Again" seminar. When you write from your heart, your topic will come alive.

Prewriting
NARROWING THE TOPIC

Once you've chosen a topic, your next step is to choose one aspect—or part of this topic— on which to focus. Use a web, like the one shown, to organize your thoughts.

Prewriting
RESEARCHING AND NOTETAKING

Make a list of questions that you want to answer in your research paper. Put each question—called a guide question—on the top of one or more note cards for use when you conduct your research.

Armed with your list of questions, you can begin the search through books, articles, and other sources. The guidelines below will help you.

Where were the camps located?

STRATEGIES FOR RESEARCHING

1. Use the card catalog or a computerized library system to find sources of information, such as encyclopedias, books, magazines, and newspapers.
2. Skim through the index or table of contents of each source to determine whether it contains the information you need.
3. Look through your sources for answers to each question. Write your findings on the appropriate note cards. State the information in your own words. If you use the exact words of a writer, use quotation marks to indicate that the words are not your own.
4. On the note card, record the author, title, and other publishing information of each source.

Prewriting
OUTLINING

Now that you have researched your topic, arrange your note cards in piles according to your guide questions. These guide questions become the main headings of your outline, designated by Roman numerals. The information in each set of cards supplies the subtopics and details under each heading. Writing a thesis statement, or main idea, for your report will help you organize your main headings and the points under them.

Here is part of the outline that student writer Tiffany Dzieginski wrote for her research paper on pages 110-111.

> Thesis Statement: Adolf Hitler, the leader of Nazi Germany, believed in the extermination of the Jewish people.
>
> I. Concentration camps
>   A. In Poland—Chelmno, Belzec, Sobibor, Treblinka, Maidanak, Auschwitz
>   B. Use of trickery to get Jews to camps
> II. Selection in the camps
>   A. Old, weak, and sick chosen for death
>   B. Healthy and strong used for slave labor

Drafting
YOUR RESEARCH PAPER

Use your outline to draft your report. Follow these guidelines.

- Introduce your paper with a question, a quotation, or a startling fact. Tiffany writes on pages 110-111, "When I was growing up, I remember staring in horror at the numbers carved on the arm of my cousin Bessie." Include your thesis statement.

- Write several supporting paragraphs that add to or develop your main idea. Each developmental paragraph needs a topic sentence and details that support it, and each roman numeral in your outline can be a supporting paragraph.

- Give credit to the authors whose ideas or words you use. Write in parentheses the author's last name and the page numbers from the book at the end of the last sentence or idea you use.

- At the end of your paper, include a Works Cited page as shown:
  Rossell, Seymour. <u>The Holocaust</u>. New York:
  Franklin Watts, 1981.

- Write a concluding paragraph that restates your main idea. Tiffany Dzieginski writes, "There but for the grace of God go I."

- Write a title for your report that, like Tiffany's title, "We Must Never Forget," captures the main idea.

Revising
YOUR RESEARCH PAPER

Read your report out loud to hear how it sounds. Are there parts that you especially like? What parts sound awkward or in need of revision? Now share your report with a partner. Does your partner understand the main idea and supporting details? Is your partner drawn into your writing? What new information has he or she learned from your report? Use this feedback and your own comments to revise your draft.

Editing
YOUR RESEARCH PAPER

After revising, work with your partner to check for errors in punctuation, spelling, and grammar. Correct your errors and make a publishable copy of your report.

Writing Workshop

Share your research by taking part in a classroom discussion entitled "Never Again." Here are some ideas for sharing:

- Begin by explaining why you picked this topic.
- Explain what you wanted to learn from your research.
- Summarize the information you learned.
- Get personal with classmates. Share your feelings about what you've learned. Point out how the study of historical events can prevent history from repeating itself.

STUDENT MODEL

We Must Never Forget
by Tiffany Dzieginski, Orland Park, Illinois

When I was growing up, I remember staring in horror at the numbers carved on the arm of my cousin Bessie. The numbers were there because Bessie was a survivor of the Holocaust. I can only imagine the terrible fear of everyday survival that Bessie and other European Jews faced because Adolph Hitler, the leader of Nazi Germany, believed in the ex-termination of the Jewish people. I wanted to find out more about Bessie's ordeal.

Thesis statement

Bessie lived in Poland. The Nazis had six death camps there—Chelmno, Belzec, Sobibor, Treblinka, Maidanek, and Auschwitz. The Nazis used trickery to get Polish Jews to go willingly to the death camps. As Nazi guards herded families onto cattle cars for transportation, they told the Jews that they were being moved to a place where there was more food and work. (Gilbert 458) The awful truth was revealed when

Facts from outline

the cattle cars reached the camps. As Jews got off the cars, Nazi officials selected who would live and who would die. They sent the old, weak, sick, and young in one direction to be killed. They kept the strong for slave labor.

The Jews selected for death did not immediately know their fate. The Nazis told them they were going to take showers. Once they entered the showers, the doors were locked and poisonous gas came out of the shower heads. Some died immediately. Others suffered for a long time. (Rossel 79)

The Jews chosen for slave labor did not live for very long. The Nazis killed them through work. Whatever work these people could produce would help the Nazis win the war. But the life of each person had no meaning. If a person was worked to death, the Nazis simply found someone else to take his or her place. "The Nazis' hatred of Jews was such that many Nazis wanted to make the Jews suffer, even more than they wanted to make money from Jewish labor. To these Nazis, slavery was better than killing the Jews immediately, for the slaves would first be profitable, then they would die, and they would also suffer cruelly." (Rossel 85)

In the camps, the Jewish laborers had very difficult lives. They received almost no food, froze in the winter, suffocated in the summer, and lived with rats, filth, and disease. And the unending knowledge of their inevitable death was always with them. (Gilbert 84)

[Paper continues.]

Somehow Bessie and others managed to survive. I remember an empty sadness in her eyes when she spoke of the camps. I always think, "There but for the grace of God go I."

Cooperative Learning

TAKE ME TO THE FAIR

If variety is the spice of life, the United States is not lacking in spice. Local newspapers often list restaurants and special events that reflect ways of life from all over the world. So set aside a date on your calendar to host a fair displaying cultural diversity.

The PROJECT

First, work as a class to prepare a list of ethnic groups or cultures that you will feature at your fair. Then divide into small groups and choose a culture from the class list that most interests members of your group. To avoid researching the same culture as another group, select one person in your group to act as a liaison. The liaison's job is make sure that there is no overlap or repetition. If there is overlap, the liaison will negotiate with other groups to work out a solution. As a last resort, the liaison can contact the teacher for help.

Assigning JOBS

Since the goal of each group is to create one booth among many, it's important to work with your group to conduct research and prepare displays. Use encyclopedias and other reference sources to find out as much as you can about the ethnic group you've chosen. Then work together to choose a topic for each group member to research. Assign topics based on the interests of group members and make a chart like the one here to help the group assign projects and make the fair work.

Project Chart

Category	Name
Music	_____
Cooking	_____
Language	_____
Sports	_____
Crafts	_____

Setting Up THE BOOTH

Setting up the booth requires cooperation and communication among group members. To make sure preparations go smoothly, assign the roles listed below.

- **Manager:** Works with group members to keep everyone on target and to maintain deadlines.
- **Materials Coordinator:** Ensures that group members have supplies, such as recipe ingredients and art materials.
- **Booth Designer:** Assembles projects and plans the layout of the booth.

Cultural FAIR DAY

Make invitations well in advance of the cultural fair and invite other classes, faculty members, parents, and community members to share in your festivities. You may want to videotape the fair in progress. If possible, play a tape recording of ethnic music at your booth. Be prepared to explain each item in your booth to guests and take time to visit other classmates and their booths.

3 Helping Your Community

AND JUSTICE FOR ALL

With a group of students, develop a campaign called "Stop." The purpose of the campaign is to make people in your community aware of injustice. To accomplish this, you and your group will make a poster with a catchy and convincing slogan.

Choosing A SLOGAN

Your slogan should be short and to the point. Most important, you want it to be memorable. Watch TV ads and look through magazines to help you generate ideas. One example of a suitable slogan is "STOP Prejudice Before It Starts."

Designing A LOGO

Create a logo that illustrates your slogan or relates to the general theme of the campaign. For example, here are some words and concepts you might show.

- **Peace**
- **Acceptance**
- **Cooperation**
- **Respect**

Creating A CAMPAIGN POSTER

Since the purpose of the poster is to make people aware of your campaign, you need to create a poster that contains the elements listed below.

- Campaign slogan
- Campaign logo
- Information about your group and what it hopes to accomplish
- Where people can find copies of your brochure (See section entitled "Writing a Brochure.")

Make your poster colorful and interesting but keep the tone serious. Get permission to hang copies in places where people will see them, such as town offices and buildings.

Writing A BROCHURE

The brochure is the heart of your campaign. It should include

- An introduction in which you describe the purpose of the campaign.
- A description of issues and attitudes that lead to an injustice such as discrimination. (Use selections from this unit to make your points.)
- Steps that people can take to stop the injustice before it begins.
- Resources that people can turn to for more information. Ask parents, teachers, and other people in your community for the names of groups, individuals, and organizations that may be helpful.

Following THE CAMPAIGN

Use the following questions to write an evaluation of your campaign. How did people in your community react to the campaign? Did your campaign reach a large audience or a small one? Was your brochure helpful? What would you do differently if you did the campaign again? What part would you do the same way if you did the campaign again?

Putting It All Together

What Have You Learned About Survival Among Various Cultures?

Now that you've finished *Unconquered*, think back about how your ideas about this theme have changed. Review your journal and other pieces of writing. Look at the projects and activities you completed. Share your thoughts with classmates by analyzing a present-day survival challenge and presenting a speech to classmates entitled "What We Can Do to Help."

SPEAKING OUT

Prewriting and Drafting   To begin, find out what's in the news. Check newspapers, magazines, and television and radio broadcasts. Talk with people in your community. Don't forget yourself. Think about the challenges that you and other young people face. Write down ideas and choose a topic that interests you personally.

Now write an outline for your speech that includes the elements listed below. For each element, prepare note cards that will jog your memory as you speak.

- An introduction about the issue and its importance to you.
- An explanation of concrete ideas and suggestions for taking action. Use the literature in this unit as a resource. For example, if you are focusing on issues of aging, review "November Serenade." If you were the daughter in this selection, what would you do to protect your father while helping him remain independent?
- A conclusion that urges others to join your crusade.

Revising and Editing   Practice your speech in front of a classmate. Is your topic clear and well defined? Do you use your note cards as prompts to refresh your memory? Do you include relevant information and suggestions?

Revise your notes and outline. Then try your speech on someone else or practice it in front of a mirror. If a tape recorder is available, use it to hear how you sound.

Publishing   To prevent nervousness, follow these suggestions on your big day:
- Speak loudly and slowly.
- Make eye contact.
- Stand up tall.
- Speak from your heart.

After you have given your speech, put it in writing. File your note cards and your speech. You may have an opportunity to present the speech again!

Evaluating Your Work

With a partner, discuss the Big Questions on pages 10-11 and the questions you generated for **Now Think!** on page 11. In your journal, write a paragraph describing how your responses to the Big Questions and to your own questions have changed after your work in this unit.

Think Back About Your Work

Flip through the pages of this text. As you flip, recall the selections you've read and the activities you've done. Take a few moments to glance through your journal. Use a critic's eye to evaluate your work. When you finish your self-evaluation, give it to your teacher. Here are some questions to guide you:

- Which literature selections in this unit affected you most strongly? Why?

- What did you learn about the ability of people to survive in the face of overwhelming obstacles?

- Which activity changed the way you felt about the plight of people in trouble?

- If you were to do one activity again, what would you do differently? What would you keep the same?

- Many selections in this unit are nonfiction; that is, the events and people are real. What do you like or dislike about reading nonfiction?

- Did you work and participate to your full potential? If not, what held you back?

Now rate your work. Use the following scale and give at least three reasons for your rating.

1 = Outstanding	3 = Fair
2 = Good	4 = Not as good as it could have been

POINT OF VIEW

What Is Point of View?

When authors write stories, they choose a **point of view**, or vantage point, from which to present the action. Many writers choose to tell their stories through the point of view of a *first-person narrator* and use the pronouns *I* or *we*. First-person narrators are characters in the story; they tell the story as they understand or experience it.

Authors who write from the *third-person point of view* use pronouns such as *she, he,* or *they*. Some writers use a *third-person limited point of view*, in which the narrator, who is usually a character in the story, tells the story through his or her eyes. Writers may also use an *omniscient*, or all-knowing, point of view. A *third-person omniscient narrator* knows everything about the actions and even the thoughts of the characters.

Comparing Points of View When a story is told through the eyes of a third-person omniscient narrator, readers are told not only what is happening but also how characters think and feel. Choose a selection from this unit in which the point of view is third-person omniscient. Retell a part of the story from the first-person point of view. Compare your retelling with the original. In a paragraph, explain how switching the point of view changes what the reader knows or learns about the character.

Telling a Story The word *omniscient* comes from two Latin words—*omnis*, meaning "all" and *scientia*, meaning "knowing." Thus, an omniscient narrator knows all there is to know about characters and events in a story. Use the omniscient point of view to write a scene from a short story. As you write, pretend that you are on a mountain top looking down at the action. Keep the definition of *omniscient* in mind as you write.

What Is Setting?

The **setting** of a work of literature is the time and place in which the action occurs. *Time* includes a specific time in history, such as 1948, or a general time period, such as past, present, or future. *Place* includes geographic location, such as the name of a country, a description of specific buildings, or the physical arrangement of a room. In some stories, the setting plays a key role in the plot. In other stories, it creates *mood*—the atmosphere or feeling created by a sense of place.

Writing about Mood   The settings of several selections in this unit refer to specific historical periods during which one group of people threatened the survival of another group. Although each of these selections has a different physical setting (for example, Poland, Vietnam, the United States) and takes place during a different time period, the mood or atmosphere of each setting is similar. Brainstorm for words, such as *tense*, *sad*, or *frightened*, that describe your feelings as you read these selections. Then write a paragraph that explains how the setting of each selection contributes to these feelings. Share your paragraph with a classmate. Notice the similarities and differences in what you wrote.

Imagining a Safe Place   Places can cause people to feel happy or sad. They can also contribute to feelings of fear or safety. Think of a real or imaginary place that makes you feel safe. Now close your eyes and picture your surroundings. Are you in a room in your house? Are you outside in a field or yard? Who is with you? A friend? A pet? No one? Is the day beginning or ending? What season of the year do you see? Describe your safe place as the setting of a short story or play.

GLOSSARY OF LITERARY TERMS

A

alliteration   Repetition of the first sound—usually a consonant sound—in several words of a sentence or a line of poetry.

allusion   An author's indirect reference to someone or something that is presumed to be familiar to the reader.

anecdote   A short narrative about an interesting or a humorous event, usually in the life of a person.

antagonist   The person or force opposing the protagonist, or main character in a literary work. [See also *protagonist*.]

autobiography   A person's written account of his or her own life.

B

ballad   A poem, often a song, that tells a story in simple verse.

biography   An account of a person's life, written by another person.

blank verse   Unrhymed poetry.

C

character   A person or an animal that participates in the action of a work of literature. A *dynamic character* is one whose thoughts, feelings, and actions are changeable and lifelike; a *static character* always remains the same. [See also *protagonist, antagonist*.]

characterization   The creation of characters through the characters' use of language and through descriptions of their appearance, thoughts, emotions, and actions. [See also *character*.]

chronology   An arrangement of events in the order in which they happen.

cliché   An overused expression that is trite rather than meaningful.

climax   The highest point of tension in the plot of a work of literature. [See also *plot*.]

comedy   An amusing play that has a happy ending.

conclusion   The final part or ending of a piece of literature.

concrete poem   A poem arranged on the page so that its punctuation, letters, and lines make the shape of the subject of the poem.

conflict   A problem that confronts the characters in a piece of literature. The conflict may be *internal* (a character's struggle within himself or herself) or *external* (a character's struggle against nature, another person, or society). [See also *plot*.]

context   The general sense of words that helps readers to understand the meaning of unfamiliar words and phrases in a piece of writing.

D

description   An author's use of words to give the reader or listener a mental picture, an impression, or an understanding of a person, place, thing, event, or idea.

dialect   A form of speech spoken by people in a particular group or geographical region that differs in vocabulary, grammar, and pronunciation from the standard language.

dialogue   The spoken words and conversation of characters in a work of literature.

drama   A play that is performed before an audience according to stage directions and using dialogue. Classical drama has two genres: *tragedy* and *comedy*. Modern drama includes *melodrama, satire, theater of the absurd*, and *pantomime*. [See also *comedy, play*, and *tragedy*.]

dramatic poetry   A play written in the form of poetry.

E

epic   A long narrative poem—written in a formal style and meant to be read aloud—that relates the adventures and experiences of one or more great heroes or heroines.

essay   Personal nonfiction writing about a particular subject that is important to the writer.

excerpt   A passage from a larger work that has been taken out of its context to be used for a special purpose.

exposition   Writing that explains, analyzes, or defines.

extended metaphor   An elaborately drawn out metaphor. [See also *metaphor*.]

F

fable   A short, simple story whose purpose is to teach a lesson, usually with animal characters who talk and act like people.

fantasy   Imaginative fiction about unrealistic characters, places, and events.

fiction   Literature, including the short story and the novel, that tells about imaginary people and events.

figurative language
Language used to express ideas through figures of speech: descriptions that aren't meant to be taken literally. Types of figurative language include *simile, metaphor, extended metaphor, hyperbole,* and *personification.*

figure of speech   A type of figurative language, not meant to be taken literally, that expresses something in such a way that it brings the thing to life in the reader's or listener's imagination. [See also *figurative language*.]

flashback   A break in a story's action that relates a past happening in order to give the reader background information about a present action in the story.

folktale   A story that has been passed along from storyteller to storyteller for generations. Kinds of folktales include *tall tales, fairy tales, fables, legends,* and *myths.*

foreshadowing   The use of clues to create suspense by giving the reader or audience hints of events to come.

free verse   Poetry that has no formal rhyme scheme or metrical pattern.

G

genre   A major category of art. The three major literary genres are poetry, prose, and drama.

H

haiku   A three-line Japanese verse form. In most haiku, the first and third lines have five syllables, while the second line has seven. The

traditional haiku describes a complicated feeling or thought in simple language through a single image.

hero/heroine   The main character in a work of literature. In heroic literature, the hero or heroine is a particularly brave, noble, or clever person whose achievements are unusual and important. [See also *character*.]

heroic age   The historical period in western civilization—from about 800 B.C. through A.D. 200—during which most works of heroic literature, such as myths and epics, were created in ancient Greece and Rome.

hubris   Arrogance or excessive pride leading to mistakes; the character flaw in a hero of classical tragedy.

hyperbole   An obvious exaggeration used for emphasis. [See also *figurative language*.]

I

idiom   An expression whose meaning cannot be understood from the ordinary meaning of the words. For example, *It's raining cats and dogs.*

imagery   The words and phrases in writing that appeal to the senses of sight, hearing, taste, touch, and smell.

irony An effect created by a sharp contrast between what is expected and what is real. An *ironic twist* in a plot is an event that is the complete opposite of what the characters have been hoping or expecting will happen. An *ironic statement* declares the opposite of the speaker's literal meaning.

J

jargon Words and phrases used by a group of people who share the same profession or special interests in order to refer to technical things or processes with which they are familiar. In general, jargon is any terminology that sounds unclear, overused, or pretentious.

L

legend A famous folktale about heroic actions, passed along by word of mouth from generation to generation. The legend may have begun as a factual account of real people and events but has become mostly or completely fictitious.

limerick A form of light verse, or humorous poetry, written in one five-line stanza with a regular scheme of rhyme and meter.

literature The branch of art that is expressed in written language and includes all written genres.

lyric poem A short poem that expresses personal feelings and thoughts in a musical way. Originally, lyrics were the words of songs that were sung to music played on the lyre, a stringed instrument invented by the ancient Greeks.

M

metamorphosis The transformation of one thing, or being, into another completely different thing or being, such as a caterpillar's change into a butterfly.

metaphor Figurative language in which one thing is said to be another thing. [See also *figurative language*.]

meter The pattern of rhythm in lines of poetry. The most common meter, in poetry written in English, is iambic pentameter, that is, a verse having five metrical feet, each foot of verse having two syllables, an unaccented one followed by an accented one.

mood The feeling or atmosphere that a reader senses while reading or listening to a work of literature.

motivation A character's reasons for doing, thinking, feeling, or saying something. Sometimes an author will make a character's motivation obvious from the beginning. In realistic fiction and drama, however, a character's motivation may be so complicated that the reader discovers it gradually, by studying the character's thoughts, feelings, and behavior.

myth A story, passed along by word of mouth for generations, about the actions of gods and goddesses or superhuman heroes and heroines. Most myths were first told to explain the origins of natural things or to justify the social rules and customs of a particular society.

N

narration The process of telling a story. For both fiction and nonfiction, there are two main kinds of narration, based on whether the story is told from a first-person or third-person point of view. [See also *point of view*.]

narrative poem A poem that tells a story containing the basic literary ingredients of fiction: character, setting, and plot.

narrator The person, or voice, that tells a story. [See also *point of view, voice*.]

nonfiction Prose that is factually true and is about real people, events, and places.

nonstandard English Versions of English, such as slang and dialects, that use pronunciation, vocabulary, idiomatic expressions, grammar, and punctuation that differ from the accepted "correct" constructions of English.

novel A long work of narrative prose fiction. A novel contains narration, a setting or settings, characters, dialogue, and a more complicated plot than a short story.

O

onomatopoeia The technique of using words that imitate the sounds they describe, such as *hiss*, *buzz*, and *splash*.

oral tradition Stories, poems, and songs that have been kept alive by being told, recited, and sung by people over many generations. Since the works were not originally written, they often have many different versions.

P

parable A brief story—similar to a fable, but about people—that describes an ordinary situation and concludes with a short moral or lesson to be learned.

personification Figurative language in which an animal, an object, or an idea is given human characteristics. [See also *figurative language*.]

persuasion A type of speech or writing whose purpose is to convince people that something is true or important.

play A work of dramatic literature written for performance by actors before an audience. In classical or traditional drama, a play is divided into five acts, each containing a number of scenes. Each act represents a distinct phase in the development of the plot. Modern plays often have only one act and one scene.

playwright The author of a play.

plot The sequence of actions and events in fiction or drama. A traditional plot has at least three parts: the *rising action*, leading up to a turning point that affects the main character; the *climax*, the turning point or moment of greatest intensity or interest; and the *falling action*, leading away from the conflict, or resolving it.

poetry Language selected and arranged in order to say something in a compressed or nonliteral way. Modern poetry may or may not use many of the traditional poetic techniques that include *meter*, *rhyme*, *alliteration*, *figurative language*, *symbolism*, and *specific verse forms*.

point of view The perspective from which a writer tells a story. *First-person* narrators tell the story from their own point of view, using pronouns such as *I* or *me*. *Third-person* narrators, using pronouns such as *he*, *she*, or *them*, may be *omniscient* (knowing everything about all characters), or *limited* (taking the point of view of one character). [See also *narration*.]

propaganda Information or ideas that may or may not be true, but are spread as though they are true, in order to persuade people to do or believe something.

prose The ordinary form of written and spoken language used to create fiction, nonfiction, and most drama.

protagonist The main character of a literary work. [See also *character* and *characterization*.]

R

refrain A line or group of lines that is repeated, usually at the end of each verse, in a poem or a song.

repetition The use of the same formal element more than once in a literary work, for emphasis or in order to achieve another desired effect.

resolution The falling action in fiction or drama,

including all of the developments that follow the climax and show that the story's conflict is over. [See also *plot*.]

rhyme scheme   A repeated pattern of similar sounds, usually found at the ends of lines of poetry or poetic drama.

rhythm   In poetry, the measured recurrence of accented and unaccented syllables in a particular pattern. [See also *meter*.]

S

scene   The time, place, and circumstances of a play or a story. In a play, a scene is a section of an act. [See also *play*.]

science fiction   Fantasy literature set in an imaginary future, with details and situations that are designed to seem scientifically possible.

setting   The time and place of a work of literature.

short story   Narrative prose fiction that is shorter and has a less complicated plot than a novel. A short story contains narration, at least one setting, at least one character, and usually some dialogue.

simile   Figurative language that compares two unlike things, introduced by the words "like" or "as." [See also *figurative language*.]

soliloquy   In a play, a short speech spoken by a single character when he or she is alone on the stage. A soliloquy usually expresses the character's innermost thoughts and feelings, when he or she thinks no other characters can hear.

sonnet   A poem written in one stanza, using fourteen lines of iambic pentameter. [See also *meter*.]

speaker   In poetry, the individual whose voice seems to be speaking the lines. [See also *narration, voice*.]

stage directions   The directions, written by the playwright, to tell the director, actors, and theater technicians how a play should be dramatized. Stage directions may specify such things as how the setting should appear in each scene, how the actors should deliver their lines, when the stage curtain should rise and fall, how stage lights should be used, where on the stage the actors should be during the action, and when sound effects should be used.

stanza   A group of lines in poetry set apart by blank lines before and after the group; a poetic verse.

style   The distinctive way in which an author composes a work of literature in written or spoken language.

suspense   An effect created by authors of various types of fiction and drama, especially adventure and mystery, to heighten interest in the story.

symbol   An image, person, place, or thing that is used to express the idea of something else.

T

tall tale   A kind of folk tale, or legend, that exaggerates the characteristics of its hero or heroine.

theme   The main idea or underlying subject of a work of literature.

tone   The attitude that a work of literature expresses to the reader through its style.

tragedy   In classical drama, a tragedy depicts a noble hero or heroine who makes a mistake of judgment that has disastrous consequences.

V

verse   A stanza in a poem. Also, a synonym for poetry as a genre. [See also *stanza*.]

voice   The narrator or the person who relates the action of a piece of literature. [See also *speaker*.]

ACKNOWLEDGMENTS

Grateful acknowledgment is made for permission to reprint the following copyrighted material.

"Unconquered and Unconquerable" by Lewis H. Latimer, from *Poems of Love and Life*.

From *The Girl in the White Ship* by Peter Townsend, copyright © 1981 by Peter Townsend. First published in the United States in 1983 by Holt, Rinehart and Winston. Reprinted by permission of the publisher.

"Mother to Son" by Langston Hughes from *Selected Poems* by Langston Hughes, copyright 1926 by Alfred A. Knopf, Inc. and renewed 1954 by Langston Hughes. Reprinted by permission of the publisher.

From *I Promised I Would Tell* by Sonia Schreiber Weitz by permission of the author. Available from Facing History and Ourselves (617-232-1595).

"We Shall Wait Forever" by Darlene Sinyella was first published in 1990 in *A Tree Full of Leaves Which Are Stars*, an anthology of Native American student poetry edited by Mick Fedullo. Reprinted by permission of the author.

"Holding Out" by Ouida Sebestyen, copyright © 1990 by Ouida Sebestyen, reprinted by permission from *Center Stage*, edited by Donald Gallo, HarperCollins Publisher.

"November Serenade" by W. J. Holmes is reprinted by permission of the author. First appeared in November 1992 issue of *Inflight Magazine*, American Air Lines.

"My People Are a Multitude of One" by Nancy Wood from *Many Winters*. Copyright ©1974 by Nancy Wood, Doubleday & Company. Used by permission.

ILLUSTRATION

14-33 Map by John Rumery; 40-59 Barbed wire by Dave Shepherd; 63-81 Petroglyphs by Dave Shepherd.

PHOTOGRAPHY

4 *t* Jim Whitmer/Stock Boston; *b* John Owens/©D.C. Heath; 5 The Museum of Modern Art, New York. Gift of Abby Aldrich Rockefeller; 6 Sarah Putnam/©D.C. Heath; 8-9 Superstock; 9 Sanjay Kothari; 10 *t* Richard Haynes/©D.C. Heath; *b* Jim Whitmer/Stock Boston; 11 *t* David Strickler/The Image Works; *c, b* Sarah Putnam/©D.C. Heath; 12 Leland Bobbe/Tony Stone Images; 13 Historical Pictures Collection/Stock Montage, Inc.; *background* Leland Bobbe/Tony Stone Images; 14 *t* Naomi Duguid/Asia Access; *bl* J.P. Laffont/Sygma; *br* Chad Slattery/Tony Stone Images; 15 *t* Jeffrey Alford/Asia Access; *b* Andrew Holbrooke/Black Star; 20 *tl* Naomi Duguid/Asia Access; *tr* Chad Slattery/Tony Stone Images; *b* Andrew Holbrooke/Black Star; 22-23 Jeffrey Alford/Asia Access; 30 J.P. Laffont/Sygma; 34-35 Patrick Deloche/Sygma; 37 Courtesy of Peter Townsend; 38 The Museum of Modern Art, New York. Gift of Abby Aldrich Rockefeller; 39 The Bettmann Archive; 40-41, 45, 48-49 State Jewish Museum, Prague; 55, 56-57 Courtesy of Sonia Schreiber Weitz; 58-59 State Jewish Museum, Prague; 59 Stuart Garfield; 60 *tl* Tom Till/Tony Stone Images; *tr* Tom Bean/The Stock Market; *bl* Tom Till/Tony Stone Images; *br* Stock Editions; 62-63, 66 Tom Bean; 71 National Anthropological Archives, Smithsonian Institution. Neg. 43, 132; 74 National Anthropological Archives, Smithsonian Institution. Neg. 3051-B; 80-81 Tom Bean; 81 *inset* Photo by Corbin Sebestyen; 82-83, 86 Hampton University Museum, Hampton, VA; 89 The Bettmann Archive; 90 *l* Frank Driggs Collection; 90-91 Lester Glassner Collection; 91 *r*, 92, 93, 97, 98 Frank Driggs Collection; 99 Courtesy of W.J. Holmes; 101 *t* National Museum of the American Indian, Smithsonian Institution, Acc. no. 3849; *b* Photo by Mary Esbaugh Hayes; 104 Nancy Sheehan/©D.C. Heath; 106 *t* J. Berndt/Stock Boston; 106 *b*, 107 Ken O'Donoghue/©D.C. Heath; 108 Ron Rovtar/FPG International Corp.; 112 *t* Sarah Putnam/©D.C. Heath; 112 *b*, 113 Kevin Thomas/©D.C. Heath; 114 *t* Rhoda Sidney/Stock Boston; *b* Images submitted to "PYE's Perfect Planet" Annual Art Contest—a project of TIMOTCA, a nonprofit, educational and charitable corporation.
Back cover *t, c, b* Sarah Putnam/©D.C. Heath.

125

Full Pronunciation Key for Footnoted Words

(Each pronunciation and definition is adapted from *Scott, Foresman Advanced Dictionary* by E.L. Thorndike and Clarence L. Barnhart.)

The pronunciation of each footnoted word is shown just after the word, in this way: **abbreviate** [ə brē′ vē āt]. The letters and signs used are pronounced as in the words below. The mark ′ is placed after a syllable with primary or heavy accent, as in the example above. The mark ′ after a syllable shows a secondary or lighter accent, as in **abbreviation** [ə brē′ vē ā′ shən].

Some words, taken from foreign languages, are spoken with sounds that do not otherwise occur in English. Symbols for these sounds are given in the key as "foreign sounds."

a	hat, cap	j	jam, enjoy	u	cup, butter	**foreign sounds**
ā	age, face	k	kind, seek	ů	full, put	Y as in French *du*.
ä	father, far	l	land, coal	ü	rule, move	Pronounce (ē) with
		m	me, am	v	very, save	the lips rounded as
b	bad, rob	n	no, in	w	will, woman	for (ü).
ch	child, much	ng	long, bring	y	young, yet	
d	did, red			z	zero, breeze	à as in French *ami*.
		o	hot, rock	zh	measure, seizure	Pronounce (ä) with
e	let, best	ō	open, go			the lips spread and
ē	equal, be	ô	order, all	ə represents:		held tense.
ėr	term, learn	oi	oil, voice		a in about	
		ou	house, out		e in taken	œ as in French *peu*.
f	fat, if				i in pencil	Pronounce (ā) with the
g	go, bag	p	paper, cup		o in lemon	lips rounded as for (ō).
h	he, how	r	run, try		u in circus	
		s	say, yes			N as in French *bon*.
i	it, pin	sh	she, rush			The N is not pro-
ī	ice, five	t	tell, it			nounced, but shows
		th	thin, both			that the vowel before
		ŦH	then, smooth			it is nasal.

H as in German *ach*. Pronounce (k) without closing the breath passage.